Celtic Fairy Tales

Dearest Conor,

    Here is the book I promised you back in the Summer. In the words of a great Scottish folk-lorist:

"It is well that each should learn the mother-song of his land at the Cradle-place of his birth." William Sharp (Fiona Macleod, 1904.)

    One day, you will live this. Meantime, enjoy our stories — they're better than the Romans!

    love,
    Aunty Fiona.
    Xmas 2008.

CELTIC FAIRY TALES

Retold with an introduction by
NEIL PHILIP

Illustrated by
ISABELLE BRENT

LITTLE, BROWN AND COMPANY

BOSTON NEW YORK LONDON

For Roisín, Sinéad, and Aisling Philip
who have Irish, Scottish, and Welsh ancestry

N.P.

For Susanna Mary Davies

I.B.

A LITTLE, BROWN BOOK
First published in Great Britain in 1999
by Little, Brown and Company (UK)

Conceived, designed and produced by
The Albion Press Limited
Spring Hill, Idbury, Oxfordshire OX7 6RU

Illustrations copyright © 1999 Isabelle Brent
Text copyright © 1999 Neil Philip
Volume copyright © 1999 The Albion Press Limited

ISBN: 0 316 64796 9

A CIP catalogue for this book is available from the British Library.

Designer: Emma Bradford

1 3 5 7 9 10 8 6 4 2

Colour origination by Culver Graphics, High Wycombe
Typesetting by York House Typographic, London
Printed in Hong Kong/China by South China Printing Co.

CONTENTS

INTRODUCTION

An Irish proverb tells us, "A tune is more precious than the song of birds, and a tale more precious than the wealth of the world." Judging from the richness of their storytelling traditions—and their music—the Celts have always believed this. To them, the world we can imagine has often seemed more real than the one in which we must live.

We can see this in the ancient Irish tales in which heroes such as Bran, son of Febal, following some mystical vision, set sail from the world of reality into the world of dream. When Bran finally sails home, no one can remember him, though he is told his name does feature in an ancient tale. When one of his men jumps down from his ship to the shore, he crumbles to ash, as if he had been dead for hundreds of years. So Bran tells the people on the shore his story and sets sail again to wander the seas forever.

Nowhere in the world is the phrase "wonder tale" more suitable for the traditional fairy tale than in Ireland and Scotland, where adults and children alike would sit around the fireside night after night as the storyteller unwound a golden thread of narrative, in words hovering on the brink of poetry. Some of the stories were short and witty, but many were long and full of adventure, infused with the transforming magic of the imagination.

Story-collector Hector Maclean described the usual setting for story-telling in the middle of the nineteenth century:

In the Islands of Barra, the recitation of tales during the long winter nights is still very common. The people gather in crowds to the houses of those whom they consider good reciters to listen to their stories. They appear to be fondest of those tales which describe exceedingly rapid changes of place in very short portions of time. . . . During the recitation of these tales, the emotions of the reciters are occasionally very strongly excited, and so also are those of the listeners, almost shedding tears at one time, and giving way to loud laughter at another.

One crofter-fisherman of Barra said that in his youth he went to listen to the same storyteller almost every winter's night for fifteen years and that he hardly ever heard the same story twice. The telling of a really complicated tale might be drawn out over as many as twenty-four evenings.

How did the storytellers remember such long, involved tales? Talking to the South Uist storyteller Donald Alasdair Johnson in 1973, folklorist D. A. MacDonald learned that Mr. Johnson visualized his stories unfolding before him, "like a film passing in front of you." He said, "You've got to see it as a picture in front of you or you can't remember it properly."

This Celtic storytelling tradition can be traced quite a long way back. An eighth-century text tells us that Mongán, son of Fiachna, king of East Ulster in the early sixth century, was told a story by his bard, Forgall, every night from Samhain to Beltane—that is, from the first of November to the first of May.

The Celts as a people had emerged by 500 B.C. as a force in central Europe; the Romans called the heartlands of the Celts Gaul, a name that still reverberates in the ancient Celtic kingdom of Galicia, now part of Spain. Gradually, the Celts were pushed to the western fringes of Europe, from where these stories come: Ireland, Scotland, Wales, the Isle of Man, Cornwall, Brittany. And they used these last dominions as a

INTRODUCTION

springboard into the new world, taking their love of stories and music to new lands: Australia, New Zealand, Patagonia, Canada, the U.S.A.

The tales in this book can only be a sampling of the treasure trove of Celtic stories. But I hope that the wonders they reveal will encourage a new generation to appreciate the great Celtic heritage of fairy tales, and to settle down of a winter's evening in the hope that the storyteller will once more say:

> There was a king and a knight, as there was and will be, and as grows the fir tree, some of it crooked and some of it straight. . . .

There is magic in those words, and magic in the air as they are spoken.

NEIL PHILIP

THE BATTLE OF THE BIRDS

THERE WAS ONCE a time when every bird was gathering to do battle. And the son of the king of Tethertown said that he would go to see the battle, and that he would bring back to his father the king word of who would be king of the birds this year.

The battle was almost over when he arrived, but the great black raven that had won the battle was being attacked by a snake, and it looked as if the snake was winning.

Without thinking, the king's son drew his sword and with one blow cut off the snake's head.

When the raven got its breath back, it said, "For your kindness to me, I will show you something. Climb up between my two wings."

The king's son mounted on the raven, and they took off. They flew over seven bens, and seven glens, and seven mountain moors.

"Now," said the raven, "do you see that house over there? Go to it. A sister of mine lives there, and she will make you welcome. If she asks you if you were at the battle of the birds, say that you were. And if she asks you if you saw me there, say you did. And be sure to meet me tomorrow, at this place."

The king's son went to the house and was given a warm welcome— anything he wanted to eat or drink, a hot bath, and a soft bed.

Next day the raven flew him once more over seven bens, and seven glens, and seven mountain moors. They came to another house, where the king's son was as well treated as before. And the next day the same thing happened again.

But on the third morning, instead of seeing the raven as before, the king's son was met by the handsomest young lad he ever saw, with a bundle in his hand. The king's son asked this lad if he had seen a big black raven, and the lad replied, "You will never see the raven again, for I am that raven. I was put under spells, and it was meeting you that freed me. Therefore I am rewarding you with this bundle. You must take it with you, staying one night at each of the three houses as before, but you must not untie the bundle until you are standing in the place where you want to live."

The king's son took his leave of the lad, and set off on the long walk home. For three nights he took lodging with the raven's sisters, as he had on the way out, and he never untied the bundle.

He was nearing his father's house when he got lost in a thick wood. It seemed to him that the bundle was getting heavier and heavier, so he decided to stop and have a look inside it.

When he untied the bundle, it unfolded and grew and swelled until it had become the grandest palace he ever saw. It was a great castle, with an orchard in which was every kind of fruit and a garden in which was every kind of herb.

He stood full of wonder and regret, for he knew it was not in his power to put the bundle back together now he had untied it, and he would have wished this magnificent house to stand in the pretty green hollow opposite his father's house.

Then he saw a giant coming towards him. "This is a bad place to build your house, king's son," said the giant.

"I know," said the king's son. "It was an accident."

"Then what reward would you give me for putting it back in the bundle as it was before?"

"What reward would you ask?" said the king's son.

"I would ask for your first son, once he is seven years old," said the giant.

"You will have him, if I have a son," said the king's son.

In a twinkling, the giant folded the castle, the orchard, and the garden back into the bundle. "Now you go your road, and I'll go my road," said the giant. "But don't forget your promise; and if you do forget, be sure that I will remember."

The king's son continued on his road and in a few days reached the green hollow of which he was so fond. Then he untied the bundle and released the castle, and the orchard, and the garden just as before.

When he went through the door, he was greeted by the prettiest girl he ever saw. "Welcome, king's son," she said. "Everything is prepared for you, if you will marry me this very night."

"I will," said the king's son, so they were married that same night.

Soon they had a son of their own, and all was well. The king's son became king in his turn, and his wife became queen. But after seven years, who should come raging to the castle but the giant. "You have forgotten your promise," he shouted. "Turn out your son."

Until now the king had not told his wife about his promise. "Leave this to me," he said. He told the giant, "You can have my son, but wait until my wife has got him ready." Meanwhile the queen dressed the cook's son in fine clothes, and led him out to the giant.

The giant went away with him, but he had not gone far when he gave the child a rod to hold. "If your father had this rod in his hand, what would he do with it?" he asked.

"He would keep the dogs and cats from going too near the king's meat," said the boy.

"You are the cook's son," said the giant, and he picked the boy up by the ankles and dashed out his brains.

The giant went back to the castle in rage and madness, shouting that if they did not send out the king's son, he would tear the castle apart stone by stone.

The queen said to the king, "We'll try again." So she dressed the butler's son in fine clothes, and led him out to the giant.

The giant had not gone far when he gave the boy a rod to hold and asked him, "If your father had this rod in his hand, what would he do with it?"

"He would keep the dogs and cats from going too near the king's bottles and glasses," said the boy.

"You are the butler's son," said the giant, and he picked the boy up by the ankles and dashed out his brains, too.

The giant returned to the castle in great rage and anger. The earth shook beneath the soles of his feet, and the castle shook, and all that was in it.

"BRING OUT YOUR SON!" the giant shouted.

So there was nothing for it but to bring out the king's true son.

When the giant asked this boy what his father would do with the rod, he replied, "Why, rule the country, of course," so the giant knew that this time he had been given the right lad.

He took the boy to his house and reared him as his own son.

One day when the giant was away from home, the king's son noticed the sweetest music he ever heard coming from a room at the top of the giant's house. When he went to look, he saw the most beautiful girl he had ever seen, playing a harp. It was the giant's youngest daughter. She beckoned him to come closer and said, "Go now, but come back at midnight; I have something to tell you."

The king's son went back at midnight, and the girl told him, "Tomorrow you will be offered the choice of my two sisters to marry, but you must refuse them, and say that you will only marry me. My father wants me to marry the son of the king of the Green City, but I don't like him.''

Next day, the giant introduced the king's son to his three daughters and said, "Now, son of the king of Tethertown, you will not lose by living with me for so long. For you may marry either of my two elder daughters, and if she agrees, go home with her the day after the wedding.''

But the king's son would not have either of the older girls. He looked straight at the youngest and said, "If you will give me this pretty one, I will be happy to marry her.''

This made the giant angry and he said, "Before you can have her, you must do three tasks for me.''

"Say on,'' said the king's son.

"First you must clean my cattle shed,'' said the giant.

"Gladly,'' said the king's son.

The giant took him to the cattle shed. "Now,'' said the giant, "the dung of a hundred cattle is in this byre, and it has not been cleaned for seven years. I am going out today, and if the byre is not sparkling clean before night comes, so clean that a golden apple will run from end to end of it and not gather a speck of dirt, then you will not get my daughter; I will drink your blood to quench my thirst tonight.''

The king's son began cleaning the byre, but he might as well have tried to bail out the ocean. By midday he was blind with sweat, and he hadn't got anywhere.

The giant's youngest daughter came out to him. "You are being punished, king's son,'' she said.

"I am,'' said the king's son.

"Come here,'' she said, "and rest awhile.''

"I might as well,'' he said, "for there is only death waiting for me whatever I do.'' And he sat down near her, and soon fell asleep.

19

When he awoke, the giant's daughter was not to be seen, but the byre was so well cleaned that a golden apple could run from end to end without gathering a speck of dirt.

The giant came back and said, "Have you cleaned the byre, king's son?"

"I have cleaned it," he said.

"Somebody cleaned it," said the giant.

"It was not you, in any event," said the king's son.

"Well," said the giant, "since you have worked so hard today, you can work even harder tomorrow. You must thatch this byre with birds' feathers, and no two feathers may be the same shade."

The king's son was out before dawn with his bow and arrows, but the birds were not so easy to kill. By midday he was blind with sweat, and he had only shot two blackbirds, and they were both the same shade.

"Come over here and rest awhile," said the giant's youngest daughter.

"I might as well," said the king's son. He sat down near her, and soon he was asleep.

When he awoke, the giant's daughter was gone. He went back to the house and saw that the byre was now thatched with feathers, each one a different shade.

When the giant came home, he asked, "Have you thatched the byre, king's son?"

"Yes, I have thatched it," he answered.

"Somebody thatched it," said the giant.

"It was not you, in any event," said the king's son.

"Well," said the giant, "as you have done so well today, we shall see how you fare tomorrow. Down by the loch there is a fir tree, and at the top of that fir tree is a magpie's nest. There are five eggs in that nest, and I want to eat them for my breakfast. Not one must be burst or broken."

So early next morning the king's son went out to climb the fir tree. From the ground to the first branch was five hundred feet. He walked round the tree and round it again, but he could not see any handhold or any foothold. He did not know what to do. He tried to climb the tree, but he could not keep a grip.

The giant's youngest daughter came to him and said, "You are rubbing the skin from your hands and feet."

"I am," he said. "I am no sooner up than down."

"Still, this is no time to give up," said the giant's daughter. She pulled off her fingers, and stuck them one by one into the tree to make a ladder for the king's son to climb to the magpie's nest.

When he reached the top, she called, "Hurry, hurry! I can feel my father's breath burning hot on my back."

In his hurry, he left her little finger in the top of the tree.

"Now, take the eggs to my father," she said. "Tonight, you will get your chance to marry me, if you can recognize me. My sisters and I will be dressed alike and will look alike. But if you love me, you will know me."

So the king's son took the eggs to the giant, and the giant said, "Make ready for your marriage."

And then there was a great marriage celebration, with feasting, and dancing until the end of the day. The giant's house was shaking from top to bottom.

When the evening came, the giant said, "Now, son of the king of Tethertown, pick out your bride."

The three daughters were dressed alike and looked alike, and there was no way to tell them apart at all. But then the king's son saw that one of the three was missing one of her little fingers, so he took her by the hand and led her to the bridal chamber.

The giant's daughter said, "Now is no time to sleep. We must flee, or my father will kill you. But I have a trick that will delay him."

She took an apple and cut it into nine pieces. She put two at the head of the bed, two at the foot of the bed, two at the door of the room, two at the door of the house, and one at the stable door. Then they took a filly from the stables, mounted up, and rode off as fast as they could.

The giant awoke and called out, "Are you asleep?"

"Not yet," called the pieces of apple at the head of the bed.

Each time the giant called out, "Are you asleep?" the next pieces of apple replied, "Not yet." But when he heard just one answer coming from the door of the stable, he knew he had been tricked. He ran upstairs to the bridal chamber, but the bed was cold, and the birds had flown.

At the mouth of the day, the giant's daughter felt her father's breath burning on her back. "Quick," she said. "Put your hand in the filly's ear, and tell me what you find."

"There is a twig of a sloe tree," he said.

"Throw it behind you," she said.

No sooner did he do that than there were twenty miles of blackthorn wood stretching behind them, so thick that a weasel could scarcely crawl through it. The giant dashed headlong into it, and soon his head and neck were being gashed by thorns.

"This is my daughter's trick," he said. "If only I had my chopper and my knife I could make short work of this." So he went home and fetched his chopper and his knife, and cut down the wood.

In the heat of the day, the giant's daughter felt her father's breath burning once more on her back. "Put your finger in the filly's ear, and throw behind you whatever you find there," she said.

The king's son pulled out a splinter of stone and threw it behind him. In a twinkling there was rock behind them, twenty miles long and twenty miles high. The giant ran slap bang into it, full pelt.

"This is my daughter's trick," he said, shaking his head. "If only I had my hammer and chisel I could make short work of this." So he went home and fetched his hammer and chisel, and broke up the rock.

At the mouth of the night, the giant's daughter once more felt her father's breath burning on her back. "Look in the filly's ear, king's son," she said, "or we are lost."

He did so, and pulled out a bladder full of water. He threw it behind him, and it became a freshwater loch, twenty miles long, twenty miles wide, and twenty miles deep. The giant came charging into it, with all the speed he could muster, until he reached the middle, and then he sank beneath the water and never rose again.

"My father is drowned," said the giant's daughter, "and will trouble us no more."

Soon they were near the king's palace. "You go home first," said the giant's daughter, "and tell your parents what has happened. Tell them about me. But while you are there, take care not to let any man or creature kiss you, for if you do you will forget all about me."

The king's son went to the palace, and everyone was overjoyed to see him. But before he could tell them about the giant's daughter, his old dog jumped into his arms and kissed him, and he forgot all about her.

The giant's daughter waited and waited by the well where he had left her, but the king's son did not come back. In the mouth of the night, she climbed up into an oak tree that was beside the well, and lay in the fork of the tree all that night.

A shoemaker lived near the well, and next morning he asked his wife to fetch some water from it. When she reached the well she looked into it and saw the reflection of the giant's daughter rippling on the surface. She thought it was her own reflection. "I never knew I was so beautiful," she said. "I'm wasted on a shoemaker." She was so taken with her own beauty that she dropped the dish she was carrying, and so went home without any water.

"Where is the water?" asked the shoemaker.

"You shambling, contemptible old fool," she answered. "Why should I slave for you, fetching you water, when with my beauty I could rule nations."

The shoemaker thought his wife must have gone mad. He asked his daughter to fetch some water, but she too saw the giant's daughter's reflection in the well and took it for her own.

When the shoemaker asked her whether she had brought him the water, she said, "Why should I fetch and carry for you, you threadbare old nobody, when with my beauty I could rule the world."

So the shoemaker had to go to the well himself. When he saw the reflection of the giant's beautiful daughter wavering over the water, he knew it was not his own. So he looked up into the oak tree and saw her there.

"Come down, my beauty," he said. "I need you to come to my house for a moment."

He led her to his house and introduced her to his wife and daughter; how sorry they were to learn that they were not so beautiful as they thought!

Then the shoemaker said, "Now I must go to the palace with shoes for the king's long-lost son, who is to be married today to his father's choice."

"I will come with you," said the giant's daughter. "I would like to see the king's son before he marries."

So they went up to the castle, and were shown into the wedding room. All the nobles were there, including the king and queen and the king's son. When the king's son saw the beautiful girl that the shoemaker had brought with him, he offered her a glass of wine.

As he poured the wine, a flame leaped up from the glass, and out of it flew a golden pigeon and a silver pigeon.

They flew about the room, and as they flew three grains of barley fell to the floor. The silver pigeon swooped and gobbled them up, and the golden pigeon said, "If you remembered how I cleaned the byre for you, you would not eat them without giving me a share."

Then another three grains of barley fell down, and once more the silver pigeon snatched them up, and the golden pigeon said, "If you remembered how I thatched the byre with feathers for you, you would not eat them without giving me a share."

Then another three grains of barley fell down, and again the silver pigeon sprang on them and ate them. "If you remembered how I helped you climb to the magpie's nest," said the golden pigeon, "you would not eat them without giving me a share. I lost my little finger doing that, and it is missing still."

The giant's daughter held out her hand to the king's son, with the little finger missing, and he clasped it in his. He remembered her then, and folded her in his arms. He kissed her on the lips, and they were married a second time. In due course they became king and queen of Tethertown themselves, and the shoemaker was rewarded with a sporran full of gold.

But never again did any son of the king of Tethertown venture to spy on the battle of the birds.

FAIR, BROWN, AND TREMBLING

THERE ONCE WERE three sisters, whose names were Fair, Brown, and Trembling. Fair and Brown had new dresses, and went to church on Sunday; Trembling wore rags, and was kept at home to do all the cooking and heavy work. They would not let her go out of the house at all, for she was so much more beautiful than the other two, they were worried she would find a husband before they did.

Fair and Brown kept on this way for seven years. At the end of that time, the son of the king of Omanya began to pay court to Fair, who was the eldest sister.

One Sunday morning, after the other two had gone to church, the old henwife came into the kitchen to Trembling and said, "You should be at church, not working here at home."

"How could I?" asked Trembling. "I have no clothes good enough to wear to church, and if my sisters were to see me there, they would kill me for leaving the house."

"I'll give you a finer dress than either of them has ever seen," said the henwife. "What would you like?"

"I would like a dress as white as snow, and green shoes for my feet," said Trembling.

Then the henwife put on her cloak of darkness, clipped a piece from the rags that Trembling was wearing, and asked for the whitest and most beautiful dress in the world and a pair of green shoes.

The moment she had the dress and the shoes, she gave them to Trembling, who tried them on. They were a perfect fit. When Trembling was dressed and ready, the henwife said, "I have a honey-bird here to sit on your right shoulder, and a honey-flower to put on your left. At the door stands a milk-white mare, with a golden saddle for you to sit on, and a golden bridle to hold in your hand."

Trembling sat on the golden saddle, and when she was ready to start the henwife told her, "You must not go inside the church, but wait at the door. The minute that people start leaving the church, you must come home as quick as you can."

When Trembling arrived at the door of the church, everyone who caught a glimpse of her was dying to know who she was. They all hurried out at the end, but they were too slow; she was already halfway home.

When she got back to the kitchen she found that the henwife had prepared the meal; all she had to do was take off her white dress and put on her rags.

When the two sisters arrived home, the henwife asked them, "Have you any news from the church?"

"Oh, yes!" they said. "The most wonderful, grand lady came to the church door. She had on the most stunning dress, and there wasn't a man in the church, from the king to the beggar, who wasn't trying to find out who she was."

Nothing would content the sisters but to have dresses just like the one that the grand lady had been wearing, though they could not have honey-birds or honey-flowers to sit on their shoulders.

Next Sunday the two sisters went to church again, in their new finery, leaving Trembling at home to cook the dinner.

After they had gone, the henwife came in and asked, "Will you go to church today?"

"I would like to go," said Trembling.

"What would you like to wear?" asked the henwife.

"A dress of the finest black satin, and red shoes for my feet."

The henwife put on her cloak of darkness and asked for the dress and the shoes. She placed the honey-bird on Trembling's right shoulder and the honey-flower on her left and sat her on the mare, with a saddle and bridle of silver.

Once again the henwife warned Trembling not to go inside the church, but to wait at the door and to rush away as soon as people rose at the end of the service.

That Sunday everyone was even more astonished than before. Everyone was looking at her and wondering who she was. But once again she slipped away so fast that no one could catch her.

The henwife had the meal ready, so all Trembling had to do was take off her satin dress and put on her rags before her sisters got home.

"What news have you today?" asked the henwife.

"We saw the grand lady again!" said the sisters. "And even our new dresses looked dowdy next to hers. Everyone was looking at her, and no one was looking at us."

So all that week the sisters gave no one any rest or peace until they got dresses as much like the lady's black satin as they could find.

On the third Sunday, Fair and Brown went to church dressed in black satin. They left Trembling at home to work in the kitchen, telling her to be sure and have dinner ready when they got back.

After they had gone, the henwife came to the kitchen and said, "Well, my dear, are you going to church today?"

"I would go if I had a new dress to wear," said Trembling.

"What dress would you like?"

"I would like a dress red as a rose from the waist down and white as snow from the waist up; a cape of green for my shoulders; a hat on my

29

head with a red, a white, and a green feather in it; and shoes for my feet with the toes red, the middle white, and the backs and heels green."

The henwife put on her cloak of darkness and asked for all these things.

When Trembling was dressed, the henwife put the honey-bird on her right shoulder and the honey-flower on her left. Then she placed the hat on her head and snipped a few hairs from one lock and a few from another with her scissors, and beautiful golden hair cascaded down Trembling's shoulders.

Trembling set off for church riding a white mare with blue and gold diamond-shaped spots all over her body and a saddle and bridle of gold. And the mare had a bird sitting between her ears, which began to sing as soon as Trembling sat in the saddle and did not stop until she came home from the church.

The fame of the beautiful lady had gone out through the world, and all the princes and great men from far and wide came to church that Sunday, each one hoping to meet her.

The son of the king of Omanya had forgotten all about Fair. All he could think about was the strange lady. So he did not go to church but hid himself outside.

The church was more crowded than ever before. Everyone was craning to get a glimpse of the beautiful lady.

As soon as they began to rise, Trembling ran from the door to the mare. She was in the saddle in an instant, and sweeping away like the wind. But the son of the king of Omanya sprang after her and caught hold of her foot. She spurred on the mare, and he was left holding her shoe in his hand.

Trembling was so upset; she thought the henwife would be very angry with her. But when she confessed, the henwife said, "Don't worry about that. It may be the best thing that ever happened to you."

When the sisters came home, Trembling was back in her rags and hard at work again.

"Have you any news from church?" asked the henwife.

"We have indeed," they said. "Today the strange lady was wearing clothes even lovelier than before, and riding the finest horse, with a little bird between its ears that was singing all the while. The lady is certainly the most beautiful that has ever been seen in Ireland."

Now after Trembling had ridden off, leaving the son of the king of Omanya with her shoe in his hand, he swore, "I will have that lady for my wife."

But the other kings' sons who had come to the church said, "Just because you have her shoe does not give you any right to her! You will have to fight us, if you want to marry her."

"When I have found her, I will fight the whole world to keep her," said the son of the king of Omanya.

So then all the kings' sons together began to travel the length and breadth of the country with the shoe, trying it on every woman in the kingdom, not caring whether she was rich or poor, or of high or low degree.

When young women saw the prince of Omanya with the shoe, many of them tried to make the shoe fit. Some cut a piece from their foot to squeeze it in; others put something extra in their stocking to bulk it out. But it was no use. The shoe was a perfectly normal size, but it just would not fit anyone but its owner; nor could anyone say what kind of material it was made from.

On the day that the princes were due to visit their house, Fair and Brown locked Trembling in the closet, "so that you will not shame us in front of the nobles."

When the prince gave the shoe to Fair and Brown they tried and tried, but they could not make it fit either of them.

"Is there any other young woman in the house?" asked the prince.

"No," said Fair.

"Yes, there is!" said Trembling from the closet. "I'm here!"

"Oh, her!" said Fair. "We only keep her to put out the ashes."

But the princes would not leave the house until they let Trembling out of the closet. When Trembling came out, she tried on the shoe, and it fitted perfectly.

The prince of Omanya looked at her and said, "You are the woman the shoe fits, and you are the woman I took the shoe from."

Fair said, "Nonsense! She's only a raggedy servant girl."

But Trembling said, "Wait here." She went to the henwife's house, and the henwife put on her cloak of darkness and wished for all the clothes again, and then Trembling put on the outfits one by one and paraded before the princes, until even Fair and Brown had to admit that she was the strange grand lady.

Then all the other princes said to the prince of Omanya, "If you want to marry her, remember you must fight us first."

"I'm ready," said the prince.

First the son of the king of Lochlin stepped forward. The struggle began, and a terrible struggle it was. They fought for nine hours, and then the son of the king of Lochlin conceded defeat.

Next day the son of the king of Spain fought for six hours; on the third day the son of the king of Greece fought for eight hours; and on the fourth day the prince fought the sons of half a dozen other kings, and defeated them all. At last there were no more princes to fight, and they all agreed that the prince of Omanya could marry Trembling.

The marriage day was fixed, and the invitations were sent out. The wedding celebrations lasted for a year and a day, and then the prince brought home his bride.

After some time, a son was born, and Trembling sent for her eldest sister to be with her and care for her. One day, when they were walking by the sea alone, Fair pushed her sister in, and she was swallowed by a whale.

Fair went home and pretended to be Trembling, for they did look very much alike.

"Where is your sister?" asked the prince.

"She has gone home, for I am quite well and don't need her any more."

"Are you sure it is not my wife that has gone?" asked the prince, for he felt in his heart that something was wrong.

"Oh, no!" she said. "It is my sister Fair that has gone."

That night the prince laid his sword between them. "If you are my wife, the sword will grow warm; if not, it will stay cold," he said.

In the morning, the sword was as cold as when he put it there.

Now although Fair and Trembling had been walking alone by the sea, they had been seen, by a young cowherd who was down by the water minding his cattle. He saw Fair push Trembling into the sea, and the whale swallow her. And next day, he saw the whales swim near the shore on the inrolling tide and cast Trembling out onto the sand.

Trembling told him, "Go and tell the prince that my sister Fair pushed me into the sea yesterday. The whale swallowed me and cast me out, but he will come and swallow me again with the next tide. He will do this three times. I am under a spell and cannot leave the beach, but must wait here to be swallowed again. Unless my husband saves me before I am swallowed for the fourth time, I shall be lost forever. He must come and shoot the whale with a silver bullet when he turns over onto his back. Under the breast-fin of the whale is a reddish-brown spot. My husband must hit him in that spot, for it is the only place in which he can be killed."

But when the cowherd got to the palace, and started to tell his story, Fair gave him a drink that made him forget it all.

Next day he went again to the sea. The whale came and cast Trembling on to the shore again. She asked the boy, "Did you tell the prince what I told you to tell him?"

"No," he said. "I forgot. The lady of the house gave me a drink, and I forgot what to say."

"Well do not forget tonight. If she offers you a drink, don't take it."

As soon as the cowherd got to the palace, Fair offered him a drink. But he refused it, and told the prince everything that Trembling had said.

Next day, the prince went down to the beach with his gun, with a silver bullet in it. He had not been there long when the whale came and cast Trembling out onto the beach. She looked at her husband, but she had no power to speak.

He kept his eye on the whale. It rolled just once onto its back, and he took aim and fired. He had but the one chance, but he took it. He hit the whale on the exact spot, and the whale, mad with pain, turned the sea all around red with its blood, and then died.

From that moment, Trembling was able to speak again. She went home with her husband, and they took the cowherd into their household, raising him as if her were one of their own, and sending him to school.

As for Fair, the prince sent her to sea in a barrel, with provisions in it for seven years.

In time, Trembling had a second child, a daughter. She said, "If this little girl lives, no one shall marry her but the little cowherd."

And so it turned out. When the cowherd and the prince's daughter got married, Trembling said to her husband, "You could not have saved me from the whale without the help of the little cowherd, so now I do not begrudge him my daughter."

The son of the king of Omanya and his wife Trembling had fourteen children, and the two lived happily until they died of old age.

THE BROWN BEAR OF THE
GREEN GLEN

IN IRELAND THERE was once a king who had three sons. John was the name of the youngest one, and he was said to be a fool.

The king fell ill. His eyes were blurred and he could not stand. So the two older brothers said that they would go to seek three bottles of the water of the Green Isle, to cure him. And they rode off on two fine horses.

The fool wanted to go too, so he saddled up an old white pony and followed them. When he got to the nearest town he found them carousing in an inn, their father forgotten. "Oh! my brothers," he said, "this is not the way to the Green Isle."

"Go home," they replied. "If you stay here pestering us, we will kill you."

"I don't want to stay with you," said John.

So he continued on his journey. At last he came to a great wild wood. Night was coming on, and the old white pony was going lame, and John began to feel frightened. So he tied the pony to the root of a tree, and climbed the tree himself.

He hadn't been perched up there long before a saw a brown bear coming with a fiery coal in its mouth.

"Come down, son of the king of Ireland," said the bear.

"Indeed I won't. I think I am safer where I am," said John.

"If you won't come down, then I must go up," said the bear.

"Do you take me for a fool?" asked John. "A shaggy, shambling creature like you could not climb a tree."

"If you won't come down, then I must go up," repeated the bear, and it began to climb slowly up, paw over paw.

"I see you can climb, after all," said John. "But there is no need. If you will stand back, I will come down to you."

So John came down to the ground, and stood talking to the bear.

"Are you hungry?" asked the bear.

"I am a little," admitted John.

The bear spun round, reached out a paw, and caught a roebuck that was passing behind him.

"Now, son of the king of Ireland," said the bear. "Would you like your share of the roebuck raw or cooked."

"Cooked, please," said John.

So the bear lit a fire, and John ate his meat cooked, while the bear ate his share raw. Then the bear said, "Lie down between my paws, and you need fear nothing until morning."

When John awoke, it was dawn. "I think we had best be going," said the bear, "for we have a long journey ahead of us. Are you a good horseman?"

"Good enough," said John.

"Climb up on me, then," said the bear.

John climbed up on the bear, but as soon as the bear made its first leap, John fell onto the earth with a thump.

"Try again," said the bear.

This time John clung on to the bear's fur with his nails and teeth, and so managed to stay on. They went for two hundred miles like this, until they came to a giant's house.

"Now, John," said the bear, "you will find this giant pretty grumpy, but you must not be afraid. Tell him that the brown bear of the green glen sent you, and he will give you food and shelter. I will come for you in the morning."

So John went into the giant's house, and the giant shouted, "Now I have you, son of the king of Ireland! If I did not get the father, I have got the son! I shall trample you into the dirt!" And he stamped his great feet on the ground.

"No you will not," said John, "for the brown bear of the green glen sent me."

"In that case," said the giant, "you shall be well cared for tonight."

The next day, the brown bear took John to a second giant's house. "This giant will be angry and try to attack you, but you must stand your ground and tell him that the brown bear of the green glen sent you."

When John went into the giant's house, the giant shouted, "Now I have you, son of the king of Ireland! If I did not get the father, I have got the son! I will blow you sky high." And the giant pursed his lips and breathed out a gale of wind that threatened to lift John right off his feet.

But John steadied himself and said, "No you will not. The brown bear of the green glen sent me."

"In that case," said the giant, "tonight you will be my guest."

The next day, the brown bear took John to a third giant's house. "This giant is the fiercest of them all," said the bear. "He will wrestle you. But if you feel he is winning, you must say, 'If the brown bear of the green glen were here, he would be your master.'"

When John went into the giant's house, the giant shouted, "Ai! Ai! Now I have you, son of the king of Ireland! If I did not get the father, I have the son!" And he leaped at John, seized him around the waist, and threw him through the door.

John and the giant wrestled among the rocks, and they attacked each other so viciously that they sank knee deep into the rock, making water gush out in springs at every step. But at last the giant got such a grip on John that he felt his back was going to break. So he called out, "If the brown bear of the green glen were here, he would be your master!"

No sooner had he spoken than the brown bear was there at his side, with his claws bared and his mouth in a snarl. And the giant said, "You have won, son of the king of Ireland. And therefore I will help you in your quest. Over there is the carcass of a sheep. Soon an eagle will come and settle on it. The eagle has a wart on its head, and you must cut off the wart with this sword without drawing a single drop of blood."

The eagle landed, and John sliced off the wart without drawing one drop of blood. Then the eagle said, "Climb up between my wings, and I will take you to the Green Isle." They flew over the ocean until they came to the Green Isle, and the eagle said, "John, be quick and fill three bottles, before the black dogs that guard the isle catch your scent."

John soon filled his three bottles from the well. But instead of going back to the eagle, he told himself that he would not go away before he had explored the isle. Beside the well was a little house, and Jack went inside it.

In the first room there was nothing but a bottle of whisky. Jack filled a glass and drank it, and then he noticed that the bottle was still as full as ever. So he said to himself, "I will take this with me."

In the second room there was nothing but a loaf of bread. Jack cut himself a slice and ate it, and then he noticed that the loaf was still whole. So he said to himself, "I will take this too."

In the third room there was nothing but a round cheese. Jack cut a slice off the cheese and ate it, and then he noticed that the cheese was still untouched. So he said to himself, "I will take this as well."

Then he went into the last room, and there he saw the prettiest little jewel of a woman he ever saw, lying asleep there. "It were a great pity not to kiss your lips, my love," said Jack, and he took a kiss from her lips.

Then the black dogs began to howl, so Jack ran back to the eagle. They flew back to the house of the third giant. The giant was collecting his rents from his tenants, and was feasting them with meat and drink. "Well, John," said the giant. "Did you ever see such an abundance of drink in your father's house?"

"I have more than that with me," said John, and he gave the giant a drink from the bottle that could never be emptied.

"I will give you two hundred notes, a bridle, and a saddle for this bottle," said the giant.

"Done!" said John. "But you must promise to give the bottle to the first sweetheart I ever had if she comes this way."

"I promise," said the giant.

Then John gave the second giant the loaf that could never be eaten, in exchange for another two hundred notes, a bridle, a saddle and the same promise, and gave the first giant the cheese on the same terms.

Then the brown bear took John back to the tree in the forest where he had left the old white pony, and John and the bear parted company.

Soon John reached the town where he had left his brothers, and he found them still carousing in the inn. He went to them and said, "I have bridles and saddles for each of us, and three bottles of water from the well of the Green Isle. Let us go home to our father."

The three brothers set off together, but as they neared home the two older ones set on John and beat him and stole the bottles of water. Then they left him for dead in a ditch and went home to boast of how they had won the healing water from the Green Isle.

While John was lying in the ditch he heard the rumble of cart wheels on the road, and he moaned, "Help me, please, whoever you are!"

It was the king's smith, with a cartload of rusty iron. The smith picked John out of the ditch and threw him in the cart, where the rusty iron rubbed against his wounds until his skin was rough and his head was bald. Then the smith said, "You can be my servant."

Now back on the Green Isle, the pretty little jewel that John had kissed woke up, and at the end of nine months gave birth to a son. "How can this be?" she asked.

"Don't worry about it," said the henwife. "Just take this bird, and go to seek the father of your son. When you find him, the bird will hop onto his head."

So first of all she ordered all the men of the Green Isle to be gathered together, and to walk in at the back door of the house and out at the front, but the bird did not stir, and the baby's father was not found.

So she said she would go around the world until she found him.

First she came to the house of the giant with the bottle. "Who gave you that?" she asked.

"John, the king of Ireland's son," said the giant.

"Well, it is mine," she said, and the giant gave it to her.

The same happened with the loaf and the cheese.

And so at last she came to the house of the king of Ireland. She explained that she was looking for the father of her son, and the king ordered all the men of Ireland to gather together, and to walk in at the back door of the house and out at the front, and they all drank from the bottle and ate from the loaf and the cheese. But the bird did not stir.

Then she asked if there was anyone else at all in Ireland who had not been through the house.

"There is only my bald, rough-skinned gillie," said the smith. "But . . ."

"Rough or not, send him here," said the girl of the Green Isle.

No sooner did the bird see the head of the bald, rough-skinned gillie than he took flight and settled on John's bald head. The sweet little jewel caught him and kissed him and said, "You are the father of my baby."

"And you are the first sweetheart that ever I had," said John.

The king was surprised to see that the bald rough-skinned gillie was none other than his foolish third son, John, who had been given up for lost. "John," he asked, "was it you who won the bottles of water for me?"

"It was," said John, and he told the king how the brown bear of the green glen had helped him find the water, and how his brothers had set upon him and left him for dead in a ditch.

"What should I do to your brothers?" asked the king.

"Cast them out," said John. "Let them eat the dust of the road and drink the muddy water from the ditch."

So the king cast out his two older sons and made John his heir, and then he gave John water from the well of the Green Isle to drink, so that his skin became smooth again and his hair grew back.

And then John married the girl of the Green Isle, and they made a rich wedding that lasted seven days and seven years, with gold a-jangling from the soles of their feet to the tips of their fingers, the length of seven years and seven days.

THE KING OF IRELAND'S SON

HERE WAS A king's son in Ireland long ago, and he went out in the snow with his gun and his dog. He killed a raven, and the raven fell onto the snow.

"I will never eat two meals at one table, or sleep two nights in one house, until I find a woman whose hair is as black as the raven's wing, whose skin is as white as the snow, and whose cheek is as red as the raven's blood," he swore.

There was only one woman like that, and she was a prisoner of the King of Poison in the eastern world.

So the next day he set out. Money was scarce, but he took twenty pounds for the journey.

He had not gone far before he came upon a funeral, and he said he would walk three steps alongside the coffin. He had not walked the three steps before a man stepped up and set down a bill on the coffin for an unpaid debt of five pounds.

The dead man's sons and daughters started weeping and wailing, because it was the law in Ireland in those days that even a dead man must pay his debts before he could be buried. When the king's son heard this, he reached into his pocket and paid the five pounds.

After that he said he would walk as far as the church. At the church gate another man set down a bill for five pounds, and the king's son said, "If I have paid one five pounds, I can pay two," and paid the debt. So now he had only ten pounds left.

He went on his way, and he had not gone far before he met a short green man who asked him where he was going. He said that he was seeking a woman in the eastern world. The short green man asked him, did he want a servant?

"Yes," said the king's son, "but I don't have much money. What wages would you be wanting?"

"The first kiss from your bride if you should win her," said the short green man, and the king's son agreed to that.

They went on their way, and had not gone far when they met another man. This man was pointing his gun into the far distance, but they could not see what he was aiming at. "What are you doing?" asked the king's son.

"I am going to shoot the blackbird that is in the eastern world, to have it for my supper," said the eyeman.

"You had better come along with us," said the short green man.

It was not long before they met another man. This one had his ear to the ground. "What are you doing?" asked the king's son.

"I am listening to the grass growing in the eastern world," said the earman.

"You had better come with us," said the short green man.

Farther along they met another man, who was herding a field of hares. This man had one leg crossed over, with the foot slung over his shoulder. "Why are you hopping about like that?" asked the king's son.

"If I unhooked this leg, I would walk so fast that I would soon be out of sight," said the footman.

"You had better come with us," said the short green man.

A while later they met another man, who was turning a windmill by snorting through one nostril; he was keeping the other nostril closed with his finger. "Why do you have your finger on your nose?" asked the king's son.

"Oh, if I were to blow with both nostrils, I would sweep the windmill right up into the air," said the blowman.

"You had better come with us," said the short green man.

Then they met another man, who was breaking stones by the side of the road. He did not have any hammer, but was breaking the stones with one of his thighs. "Why are you doing that?" asked the king's son.

"If I used both my thighs, I would grind the stones to powder," said the thighman.

"You had better come with us," said the short green man.

So the son of the king of Ireland, the short green man, the eyeman, the earman, the footman, the blowman, and the thighman, all went forward together, until the evening came, and the end of the day.

They came to the house of a giant, and the short green man said, "We shall stop here tonight."

He went up to the door and rat-tat-tatted with his stick.

The giant came to the door, saying, "I feel the smell of a melodious lying Irishman in the air."

The short green man said, "I am no melodious lying Irishman. I am come to tell you that my master is coming, and that if he finds you here he will strike your head off." As he spoke, the short green man was growing bigger, and bigger, and bigger, until he was nearly the size of the giant's house.

"Is your master as big as you?" asked the giant fearfully.

"Bigger," said the short green man.

"Help me hide until the morning," begged the giant.

So the short green man put the giant under lock and key and went back to tell the king's son that the coast was clear.

The son of the king of Ireland, the short green man, the eyeman, the earman, the footman, the blowman, and the thighman, spent the night in the giant's castle, one third of it telling fairy tales, one third of it telling tales of the hero Finn MacCool, and one third of it in sweet slumber.

In the morning they left, and the short green man went back to release the giant. But before he would undo the lock, he asked the giant to give him the old black cap that was under his bed.

"I will give you a brand new top hat I have never worn," said the giant. "I would be ashamed to give you the old black cap."

But the short green man insisted. "If you don't give me the old black cap, my master will come back and strike your head off."

"In that case I shall give it to you," said the giant.

The short green man undid the lock, and the giant gave him the old black cap, saying, "If you put this on your head, you can see everyone, but no one can see you."

The next night they spent at a second giant's house, one third of the night in telling fairy tales, one third in telling tales of Finn MacCool, and one third in sweet slumber. This time when they left, the short green man asked the giant for the old slippers that were under his bed. The giant offered him a pair of new boots, but he insisted, and the giant told him, "If you put on these slippers and say 'high-over,' they will take you anywhere you want."

The next night they spent at a third giant's house, one third of the night in telling fairy tales, one third in telling tales of Finn MacCool, and one third in sweet slumber. This time, the short green man asked the giant for the rusty sword that was under his bed.

"I would not give that sword to anyone," said the giant.

But the short green man insisted. "If you don't give me the rusty sword, my master will come back and strike your head off."

"You shall have the sword," said the giant. "It will cut through anything, even iron, and will not stop until it touches the earth."

So the king of Ireland's son, the short green man, the eyeman, the earman, the footman, the blowman, and the thighman, went forward again until evening came, and the end of the day. And that night they arrived in the eastern world, where lived the lady with hair as black as a raven's wing, skin as white as snow, and cheeks as red as blood.

The king's son and his companions got lodgings in the castle of the King of Poison, where the lady was. The castle was all set around with skulls on spikes.

"What do you want?" asked the lady.

"I want to marry you," said the king's son.

"If you want to marry me, you must free me from enchantment," said the lady. "But I must tell you, all the skulls that you see around the castle walls are the skulls of men who have tried to set me free. If you fail, your skull will join theirs."

"I am not afraid," said the king of Ireland's son.

So the lady gave him a pair of scissors. "This is the first test," she said. "You must give those scissors back to me in the morning."

"That is not much of a test," said the king of Ireland's son.

But in the night the lady placed a pin of slumber under his pillow, so that as soon as he went to bed he fell fast asleep, and then she came and took the scissors, and gave them to the King of Poison.

If the short green man had not been keeping watch, the king's son would have been lost. But the short green man put the old black cap on his head, and the old slippers on his feet, and took the rusty sword in his hand, and said "high-over," and in a flash found himself in the room of the King of Poison. He took the scissors back and gave them to the king's son.

In the morning, the lady asked, "Do you have my scissors?"

And the king's son replied, "Yes, lady, I have."

So next night she gave him a comb and said that he must give it back to her in the morning. Again she set the pin of slumber under his pillow, stole back the comb, and gave it to the King of Poison. Again the short

green man put on his hat, his slippers, and his rusty sword, and stole it back.

In the morning when the king's son awoke he felt for the comb, but it was gone. "I've lost it!" he cried.

But the short green man said, "Don't worry, I have it."

And when the king's son gave the lady the comb, she was full of wonder.

On the third night, she said to the son of the king of Ireland. "Tomorrow morning, you must give me the head of the man who cuts his hair with the scissors and combs his hair with the comb. If you do not, you must lose your own head."

That night she gave the scissors and the comb to the King of Poison, and told him to guard them with his life. So the King of Poison hid them inside a great stone, and locked it behind three score locks, and sat beside it all night long.

The lady set the pin of slumber under the pillow again, and the king's son fell fast asleep. But the short green man put on his old black cap, and his old slippers, and his rusty sword.

"High-over!" he said, and in an instant he was beside the great stone. He could see the King of Poison, but the King of Poison could not see him, because he was wearing his cap of invisibility.

The short green man drew the rusty sword. With his first stroke he cut through the locks; with his second stroke he cut through the stone; and with his third stroke he cut off the King of Poison's head.

When the short green man returned, he woke the king's son and gave him the head, the scissors, and the comb.

In the morning, the lady came and asked, "Do you have the head?"

And the king's son replied, "I have the head, and the scissors, and the comb," and he threw her the head of the King of Poison.

The lady gave out a great shriek of anger. "I will never marry you unless you can send a runner who will fetch three bottles of the water of life from the well of the western world, and fetch them quicker than the runner I will send. If my runner comes back first, you must lose your head."

The lady sent for an old hag, and gave her three empty bottles to fetch water from the well of the western world. The short green man asked for three bottles to be given to the footman who had been herding the field of hares.

The footman and the hag set off together. The footman unhooked his foot from over his shoulder, and soon he was out of sight. He got to the well of the western world, filled his bottles, and was halfway home while the hag was only halfway there.

He greeted her, and she said, "Sit down and rest awhile. They are already married, so there's no need to break your heart running." So he settled down, and she put a slumber pin under his head, so he fell asleep. Then she spilled out the water of life from his bottles and went on her way.

The short green man said, "The footman is a long time coming. Earman, put your ear to the ground and tell me what is happening."

"I can hear the hag coming," said the earman, "but the footman is fast asleep; I can hear him snoring."

So the short green man asked the eyeman to see if he could see where the footman was.

"He is lying asleep by the road, with a slumber pin under his head."

"Put your gun to your eye and shoot the pin away."

The eyeman put his gun to his eye and shot the pin from under the footman's head. The footman woke with a start and saw that his bottles were empty and he must go back to the well. As he set off, he was passed by the hag, on her way back to the castle.

The eyeman said, "The hag is coming."

The short green man said to the blowman, "Try to stop her."

The blowman blew out of his right nostril. It buffeted the hag, but she kept on coming. He blew with his left nostril. It swayed the hag, but she kept on coming. At last he blew with both nostrils and sent her sailing through the air, all the way back to the well of the western world.

The footman came running up with the three bottles of water, and the son of the king of Ireland had won the race.

The lady let out another shriek of anger. She said, "I will never marry you until you have walked three miles without shoes or stockings over sharp steel needles." And she had sharp needles set point up over a road three miles long.

The short green man said to the thighman, "Go and blunt those." The thighman went along them with one thigh and reduced them to stumps; he went along them with two thighs and reduced them to powder. And the king of Ireland's son walked along the road as free and easy as a fine young lad on a country stroll.

So he had won his wife with hair as black as a raven's wing, skin as white as snow, and cheeks as red as blood.

They were married then, and the short green man said, "Don't forget, I am to have the first kiss."

So the short green man kissed the bride, and all the poisonous serpents that the King of Poison had put in her with his spells came out of her mouth; if the king's son had kissed her, he would have been bitten to death.

Then the short green man said to the son of the king of Ireland, "You can go with your wife now. I am the man who was in the coffin that day when you paid the ten pounds so that my body could be buried. These others are servants whom God has sent to you, to repay your kindness."

Then the short green man, and the eyeman, and the earman, and the footman, and the blowman, and the thighman went away, and the son of the king of Ireland never saw them again.

He brought his wife home, with her hair black as a raven's wing, her skin white as snow, and her cheeks red as blood, and they spent a happy life with one another.

THE THREE BLOWS

NCE UPON A time there was a farmer in south Wales who took his sheep to graze near Llyn y Fan Fach, a lovely lake in the Black Mountains. His name was Myddfai.

When he looked out over the lake, Myddfai saw a beautiful maiden standing on the surface of the lake, combing her golden hair and studying her reflection in the glass-smooth water.

Entranced by her beauty, Myddfai walked to the water's edge. He held out his hand to the beautiful maiden, offering her all he had to give, which was an old dry crust of bread. But she said the bread was too hard, and fled across the water.

Next day he tried again, with bread that was only half baked, but this time she said the bread was too soft, and fled once more.

On the third day, he offered her a perfect new-baked loaf, and she said:

> Well-baked is your bread;
> With you I'll be wed.

Myddfai was overjoyed, and he did not pay much attention when she added, "But if you ever strike me three causeless blows, you shall lose me forever."

The fairy disappeared beneath the lake, and when she reappeared there were three of her, or so it seemed, for she had brought her two sisters with her. "Which of us is which?" they asked. But Myddfai was trained to tell one sheep from another, or one cow from another, so he noticed little details. He saw that one of the girls had a wider sandal strap than the others and knew that that one was his true love.

She stepped forward and called forth from the lake seven cows, two oxen, and one bull as her dowry.

For four years they lived happily together, and they had three sons. Then one day they were invited to a christening, and in the middle of this happy event, the fairy wife burst into floods of tears. Her husband gave her an angry look. "Control yourself," he said, and he nudged her with his arm.

"That is one causeless blow," she said. "I was crying because that poor baby is entering a world of pain and sorrow; why should I not cry?"

And true enough, after a short while the baby died, and they were invited to its funeral. At the funeral, the fairy wife burst into happy laughter, and the husband nudged her again, saying, "Stop it."

"That is two causeless blows," she said. "I was laughing because that dear baby has no more misery to endure; it has gone to a happy land. Why should I not laugh?"

Soon after, they were invited to a wedding. The bride was young, pretty, and poor, and the husband was old, ugly, and rich.

As the bride said, "I do," the fairy wife burst once more into uncontrollable tears.

Her husband was so embarassed, he said "Keep quiet, please."

But she said, "Youth marries age for greed, not love; why should I not cry?"

He nudged her with his arm, "Everyone is looking!"

"Well they have looked their last," she said, "for that was the third causeless blow. You have lost me forever, and you will never see me again. Farewell, husband, farewell."

She went back to the lake, and took with her the seven cows, the two oxen, and the bull that had been her dowry. The oxen were at that moment plowing in the field, but they left off their work and followed her call, dragging the plow behind them and leaving a furrow which can still be seen leading down into the waters of the lake.

Only once more was the fairy of the lake seen above the water. One day when her three sons were grown, they went down to the lake and called for their mother. She appeared to them and gave them a magical box containing healing remedies of great power. And the three sons and their sons and daughters after them are renowned to this day as the celebrated physicians of Myddfai.

RORY THE FOX

NE DAY, RORY the fox saw a fine rooster and a fat hen and thought they would make a good supper. But as soon as they saw him, they jumped up into a tree.

Rory did not lose heart but went up to talk to them. "There's no need to be afraid of me," he said. "Haven't you heard? Peace has been declared between all the animals, and even between animals and men. To celebrate, let's go for a stroll together."

The rooster said, "What wonderful news! But wait!" He turned to the hen. "Are those hounds I see coming across the field?"

"Yes," replied the hen. "They'll be here any minute."

"If that is the case," said Rory, "perhaps I should be off. For I am afraid the hounds may not have heard about the peace yet."

And with that the sly fox took to his heels and never drew breath till he reached his den.

Another day, Rory the fox saw a fine fat goose asleep by the side of a loch, so he pounced and seized her by the wing.

The goose made a great hissing and commotion, and Rory said, "What's all the fuss about? If you had me in your mouth, as I have you, what would you do?"

"That's easy," said the goose. "I would fold my hands, shut my eyes, say a grace, and then I would eat you."

"And that's exactly what I am going to do," said Rory. He folded his hands, put on a pious face, closed his eyes, and said a grace.

While he did so, the goose spread her wings and flew off across the loch, cackling with glee, and poor Rory was left to lick his lips for his supper.

"Let that be a lesson to me," he said, "never to say grace before the meat is in my belly."

One day, Rory the fox met a rooster, and they fell to talking.

"How many tricks can you do?" asked the fox.

"I can do three," said the rooster. "How many can you do?"

"I can do seventy-three," said the fox.

"Such as?" said the rooster.

"I can close my eyes and give a great shout," said the fox.

"Even I can do that," said the rooster, and he shut his eyes and crowed as loud as he could. While he was doing that, the fox gripped him by the neck and ran away with him.

As they passed the farm, the hen saw them and shouted, "Let go of the rooster; he's mine!"

"Say, 'No he's not, he's mine now,'" said the rooster.

So the fox opened his mouth to say it, but the rooster jumped clear and sprang to the rooftop, where he shut his eyes and crowed with all his might:

Cock-a-doodle-do!
I've got away from you.

LUTEY AND THE MERMAID

UNDREDS OF YEARS ago, there lived near Lizard Point in Cornwall a man named Lutey, who farmed a few acres of land along the seashore, and supplemented his income by a bit of fishing and a bit of smuggling when the time was right.

One summer's evening, he was returning home from the cliff, where he had spent a day cutting turf, when he decided to go down to the shore and see if the sea had cast up any treasures from a shipwreck. But there was nothing worth picking up.

Lutey was about to give up when he heard a thin high sound, like the wailing of a woman or the crying of a baby, which seemed to come from the sea. Going in the direction of the cry, he came to a rock pool, in which he saw the most beautiful woman he had ever seen. Only her head and shoulders were visible; the rest of her was draped in seaweed or submerged beneath the water. Her golden hair tumbled over her shoulders and floated on the water, like sunbeams on the sea. Her skin was as smooth and clear as a polished shell.

She was looking out at the retreating tide and crying her piteous cry. Lutey wished he could help her. Not wishing to frighten her, he coughed to let her know she was there, and she let out an unearthly yell.

"Don't be afraid of me," he said. "I'm a married man, near thirty years old. My name is Lutey. What can I do to help you, my turtle dove? Believe me, I wouldn't hurt you for the world."

He carried on talking like that, gentle and low, and at last the woman

60

stopped crying. She looked at him, and her eyes shone like bright stars on a dark night. Lutey drew closer to her, and it was then that he saw beneath the waters of the pool the shadow of a fish's tail, quivering and shaking among the seaweed, and knew that she was a mermaid. He had never seen one before, though he had heard them singing on moonlit nights, across the water.

"Now, my lovely maid of the waves," he said, "tell me what I can do for you. Speak to me; or, if you do not know our Cornish tongue, give me a sign."

"We people of the ocean can speak all tongues," said the mermaid, "for we visit the shores of every country, and all the peoples of the world sail over our domain."

She rose out of the water and seated herself on a rock. Her golden hair was so long and full that if fell around her like a glittering robe.

"Only three hours ago," she said, "I left my home beneath the sea to come and gaze over the land, where I can never go, though I long to see its wonders. And now, through my foolishness, I have been trapped here by the tide. If you will help me back to the sea, I will grant you any three wishes your heart desires." She took from her hair a golden comb with a pearl handle and gave it to Lutey, saying, "Here, take this as a token of good faith. If you ever need my help, you need only pass that comb through the sea three times and call my name, and I will come to you."

"What is your name?" asked Lutey.

"It is Morvenna," she answered, which in Cornish means "sea-woman."

Lutey was a strong man, so he picked the mermaid up and carried her out to sea. While he walked across the sand with his strange burden, he struggled to recall every story he had ever heard of those who had been granted wishes. He remembered the man who wished that all he touched

62

would turn to gold, and how badly that had turned out.

When they reached the sea, the mermaid said, "Come, there is no time to waste. What are your three wishes? Do you wish for long life, strength, and riches?"

"No," said Lutey. "I wish for power to do good. Therefore, my first wish is that I should be able to break the spells of witches; my second wish is that I should have power to make spirits tell me anything I need to know for the benefit of others; and my third wish is that these good gifts should be passed down in my family forever."

The mermaid promised that his wishes should come true.

Lutey waded out with her until the water was up to his waist, and as they walked she told him of the wonders of her life beneath the ocean. "Our walls are made of coral and amber, and our floors are strewn with pearls. The roof shines with diamonds and makes our home as bright as day." Flinging both arms around Lutey's neck, she implored him, "Come with me, love, and see it all for yourself."

Lutey was very tempted, for he was more than half under her spell. "I would love to go," he said, "but I should be drowned."

"No," she said, "for with my magic I could make you gills, so that you could breathe under water. And when you get tired of life beneath the sea, you can always return to the land, and take with you as many treasures as you can carry. So come along, love."

The mermaid's eyes sparkled as she saw that she had Lutey in her power. But just then Lutey's dog Venture, left forgotten on the shore, began to bark, and Lutey looked round and saw his little house, with the smoke curling from the chimney, and the mermaid's spell was broken. He struggled to free himself from her embrace, but she kept her arms clasped around his neck, crooning, "Come with me, love. Come with me."

Lutey drew his knife, and the cold steel forced the mermaid to drop from his neck into the sea. She swam away, but she was still singing, "Farewell, my love, for nine long years, and then I'll come for thee."

Lutey barely had the strength to stagger back to the shore, where he fell down among the rocks in a swoon.

Next morning, Lutey's wife, who was very worried about her husband, came down to the shore to look for him and found him slumbering there. She shook him awake, saying, "What are you doing down here?"

When Lutey came to, he didn't know where he was, on the land or under the sea. "Are you my lovely Morvenna?" he asked. "You don't look like her."

"No indeed," said his wife. "I am Betty Lutey, as you well know, and I've never heard of this lass you're dreaming of."

"Well if you are my wife, you have had a lucky escape," said Lutey, and he told her everything that had happened. To prove it was true, he gave her the comb that the mermaid had given him.

Lutey asked his wife not to tell anyone what had happened, but that was too much to expect of anyone, and soon the whole countryside knew about Lutey's adventure with the mermaid, and the three wishes she had granted him.

Soon people who were suffering from witch's spells or needed help in some other way were flocking to the new pellar, or conjurer. And although Lutey had had to force the mermaid to let him go, he found that she had been as good as her word, and he could both break spells and find out information from spirits, as long as it was to help and not to harm.

Yet Lutey paid dearly for his new skills. Nine years later, to the very night, he went out fishing with a friend. It was a clear moonlit night, and the sea was as smooth as glass. Suddenly, there was a rippling, and the sea rose around the boat. In the curling waves was the mermaid,

Morvenna, with her golden hair streaming behind her over the water.

"My hour is come," said Lutey, and he plunged into the sea. He swam out with the mermaid for a little way, and then they sank beneath the waves, and the sea became as smooth as before.

Lutey's body was never found.

His descendants did inherit his powers, but also his curse. For, every nine years, one of them finds a grave in the sea.

"GIVE ME A CRAB, JOHN"

N THE ISLE of Man, mermen are said to be very fond of crabs. One day, an old man was down on the shore looking for crabs and found a great number. He saw a merman out in the sea who was also looking for crabs, but who hadn't found any.

The merman sang to him, "Give me a crab, John."

"What will you give me for it?" the old man shouted back.

"I'll tell your fortune," said the merman.

So the old man threw him a couple of crabs, and the merman caught them.

As the merman sank back beneath the waves, he sang the old man's fortune: "As long as you live upon the land, you will never be drowned in the sea."

THE BLACK BULL OF NORROWAY

I N NORROWAY, LONG ago, there lived a lady, and she had three daughters.

The oldest of them said to her mother, "Mother, bake me a bannock and roast me a collop, I'm going away to seek my fortune." Her mother did so, and the daughter went to the witch washerwoman to ask her advice.

The washerwoman said, "Stay with me, and keep watch out of the back door, and see what you shall see."

She saw nothing the first day, and nothing the second day. On the third day, she saw a coach-and-six coming along the road. She ran in and told the washerwoman. "Well," said the washerwoman, "that's for you." So she got into the coach, and drove off.

Then the second daughter said to her mother, "Mother, bake me a bannock and roast me a collop, I'm going away to seek my fortune." Her mother did so, and the daughter went to the witch washerwoman to ask her advice.

She kept watch out of the back door as her sister had done. On the third day, she looked out and saw a coach-and-four coming along the road. "That's for you," said the washerwoman, so she got into the coach, and drove off.

At last the third daughter said, "Mother, bake me a bannock and roast me a collop, I'm going away to seek my fortune." Her mother did so, and the daughter went to the witch washerwoman to ask her advice.

The washerwoman told her, "Look out of the back door, and see what you shall see."

She saw nothing the first day, and nothing the second day. The third day she looked again.

"What can you see?" asked the old witch washerwoman.

"Nothing but a great black bull coming roaring up the road."

"Well," said the washerwoman, "that's for you."

On hearing this the girl was nearly distracted with grief and terror, but she was set on the bull's back, and away they went.

They went on and they went on until the girl was faint with hunger. "You will find food in my right ear, and drink in my left ear," said the black bull. So she did as he said, and was wonderfully refreshed.

At last they came in sight of a fine castle. "We must get there tonight," said the bull. "My eldest brother lives there."

When they arrived at the castle, she was lifted off the bull's back and taken to a bedchamber, while the bull was taken to a paddock.

The next morning, the bull's brother, who was a handsome man, took the girl into a fine shining room and gave her a beautiful apple, telling her not to break it until she was in the worst trouble any mortal ever was in, and it would save her.

Then she was lifted on to the bull's back, and they continued their journey. When she had ridden far and farther than I can tell, they came in sight of an even grander castle, the home of the bull's middle brother. The same thing happened again, except this time the girl was given the finest pear ever seen and told not to break it until she was in the worst trouble any mortal ever was in.

On the third day, they rode to the grandest castle of all, the home of the bull's youngest brother. And here the girl was give a luscious plum and told not to break it until she was in the worst trouble any mortal ever was in.

Next day they rode on, far, far, and farther still, until they came to a dark and fearsome glen. Here they stopped, and the girl got down from the bull. The bull said, "Here you must stay, while I go and fight the devil. Sit on this stone, and do not move a hand or foot until I come back, or I will never find you again. If everything about you turns blue, then I have beaten the devil. But if everything turns red, he will have conquered me."

She sat herself down on the stone, and by and by everything around her turned blue. She was so full of joy that she lifted one foot and crossed it over the other. So when the bull returned, he could not find her.

She sat and waited, but the bull never came. Long she sighed and long she cried, and at last she gave up hope and wandered off. She did not know where she was going.

On she wandered, until she came to a great hill of glass. She tried to climb it, but she couldn't. So she tried to go round it, but she couldn't. At last she came to a smith's house, and the smith told her that if she worked for him for seven years, he would make her a pair of iron shoes so that she could climb the glass hill.

She worked for seven years, and at the end of that time she had earned her iron shoes. She climbed the glass hill, and at the top of it she came to the house of the old witch washerwoman.

There she was told of a young knight who had given in a bloody shirt to be washed, saying that whoever could remove the bloodstains should be his wife. First the old witch washerwoman had tried, and then her daughter had tried. They had washed the shirt and washed it and washed it again, but they could not get the stains out.

They gave the bloody shirt to the girl, and she set to work. As soon as she put the shirt in the water, the stains vanished, and the shirt was pure and clean.

The old witch washerwoman sent the shirt back to the handsome knight, saying that her daughter had cleaned them; so it was arranged that the daughter and the knight should be married.

When the girl who had actually cleaned the shirt saw the knight she fell in love with him at first sight. And somehow she knew that the knight was none other than her own black bull. She did not know what to do. Then she remembered the apple she had been given. She broke it, and found it was filled with gold and jewels, the richest she had ever seen.

She said to the washerwoman's daughter, "I will give you these jewels, on condition that you put off your marriage by one day, and allow me to go into his room alone at night."

The washerwoman's daughter agreed, so that night the girl went into the knight's room. But the washerwoman had prepared a sleeping drink for him, and he was sound asleep.

All night the girl sat by his side, sobbing and singing:

> Seven long years I served for thee,
> The glassy hill I climbed for thee,
> The bloody shirt I washed for thee—
> Will you not waken and turn to me?

Next day she was in despair. She broke open the pear, and found it filled with jewels even richer than the contents of the apple. So she bargained with the washerwoman's daughter for another night in the young knight's chamber. But once again the washerwoman had given him a sleeping drink, so although she sat by his side, sobbing and singing all night long, he never woke.

On the next day, the young knight went out hunting, and one of his companions asked him what the noise and crying was that they had heard all night from his bedchamber for the last two nights. He said he had not heard any noise; but he resolved to stay awake the next night.

The girl broke open the plum, and found it held the richest jewels of all. She gave them to the washerwoman's daughter in return for one more night's reprieve.

And that evening, when the washerwoman gave the young knight the sleeping drink, he said, "This is very bitter. Could you fetch me some honey to sweeten it?" And while the old witch was away fetching the honey, he poured the drink away and only pretended to have drunk it.

That night the girl crept once again into the young knight's room. She sat by his side, and sang:

> Seven long years I served for thee,
> The glassy hill I climbed for thee,
> The bloody shirt I washed for thee—
> Will you not waken and turn to me?

And he heard, and turned to her.

She told him everything that had happened to her, and he told her all that had happened to him, and how he had been enchanted into the shape of a black bull until he could find a girl to love him, and beat the devil.

And he and she were married, and are living happy to this day, for all I know.

FINN MacCOOL AND THE SCOTTISH GIANT

STRONG-ARM FINN had lived all his life without ever meeting his match, so he was as proud as a peacock. He never did any work, but just played at games with his warriors and threw great stones about. He left his wife Oonagh at home while he enjoyed himself.

Well, one day Finn was quite down in the mouth, because he had no one to wrestle with, and no rocks to throw. So when he saw a man running towards him, he shouted, "What's in the wind?"

"It's Far Rua, the Scottish giant. He's heard tell of you and your strength, and now he's coming this way to match himself against you."

Well, Finn had heard tell of Far Rua too. When Far Rua stamped, the whole of Scotland shook. The fame and name of him went far and near. He had a magic finger that gave him tremendous strength. Once he had flattened a thunderbolt with one blow of his fist; he kept it in his pocket in the shape of a pancake.

So when Finn heard the man's news, he was seized with a very warm and sudden fit of affection for his wife, poor woman, so he pulled up a fir tree, lopped off its roots and branches, took it for a walking stick, and set off for home.

Finn and Oonagh's house was built right on top of a mountain. There wasn't enough water on the mountain, and there was too much wind. But there was just the right amount of view: lots of it, in every direction.

When Finn got home, Oonagh gave him such a kiss the water of the lake below curled with the pleasure of it. But Finn just groaned.

"What's the matter, my darling bully?" said Oonagh.

"It's that Far Rua," said Finn. "He's coming. He'll be here soon. He's got a magic finger that gives him all his strength. He'll flatten me like he did that thunderbolt."

"We'll see about that," said Oonagh, and she began to prepare for the giant's visit.

When she saw Far Rua coming, Oonagh tucked Finn up in the cradle. "You can be a baby again," she said, "and I don't expect to hear more than a gurgle pass your lips without my leave."

When Far Rua arrived, he asked, "Is this Finn's house? I've come all the way from Scotland to fight him."

"Finn's not at home," said Oonagh. "He's gone to teach that fool Far Rua a lesson. I do hope for Far Rua's sake that Finn doesn't find him."

"I am Far Rua," said the giant, "and Finn has been avoiding me these last twelve months. I can't wait to get to grips with him."

Oonagh let out a great laugh. "You've never seen Finn, then?"

"How could I?" said Far Rua. "He's so spry at dodging me."

"I thought you couldn't have seen him," Oonagh replied. "And if you take my advice, you poor-looking creature, you'll pray night and day that you never do see him."

Far Rua didn't look very happy at this.

"Anyway," Oonagh continued, "as Finn is away from home just now, perhaps you would do me a kindness. The wind is whistling in at the door. If my Finn were here, he would turn the house around for me."

Far Rua wasn't going to be outdone by Finn, so he cracked the middle finger of his right hand three times, and put his arms around the house, and heaved. The whole house turned round like a spinning top, and in his cradle Finn let out a little whimper.

"How kind," said Oonagh. "Perhaps while you're about it you could do me another kindness. If my Finn were here he would pull the rocks of the mountain aside to make me a new well. I'm sure there's fresh spring water down there."

Far Rua looked at the mountain, cracked the middle finger of his right hand nine times, put his arm around a rock, and heaved.

There was a great *crack!* and a shower of water burst forth from the new well.

"How kind," said Oonagh. "Now, do come in and have a bite to eat."

With that, Oonagh handed Far Rua a griddle cake with the griddle baked inside it. Far Rua put it in his mouth to take a huge whack out of it and "Blood and fury!" he cried. "The two best teeth in my head are gone."

"Oh dear," said Oonagh, as mild as the moon. "Try some steak to soothe your gums." And for a steak she gave him a plank of red pine wrapped round with a scraping of meat.

When Far Rua bit into the steak, his teeth stuck fast in the wood, and he could barely get them out again.

"By my sword, ma'am," he said, "this is a hard diet you give your guests."

"Hard?" said Oonagh. "Why, it's the same food we give the baby." And she gave Finn in the cradle an ordinary griddle cake and a genuine steak, and he took a great bite from both.

I'm lucky Finn's not at home, thought Far Rua, *if even his baby can munch food that splinters my teeth.*

"I'd like to take a look at this child," he said.

"By all means," said Oonagh. "Get up, dear, and show this decent little man something that won't be unworthy of your father, Finn."

So Finn got up from the cradle in his baby clothes and handed Far

Rua a stone from the hearth. "Can you squeeze water out of that?" he asked.

Far Rua cracked his finger, and squeezed, but not even he could wring water from a stone. He passed the stone to Finn, and Finn secretly slid it behind him and instead picked up a loaf set to rise by the fire. He squeezed, and water oozed out in a little shower from his hand.

"I'll not bandy words with anyone that can't eat my mammy's bread, or squeeze water out of a stone," he said, and he climbed back into his cradle.

"I must see what sort of grinders that baby's got to eat griddle bread like that," said Far Rua.

"You'll have to put your finger to the back of his mouth to find his teeth," said Oonagh.

So Far Rua chucked the baby under the chin, and put the third finger of his right hand in its mouth.

Snap!

Finn's mouth shut, his teeth chopped off the giant's finger, and Far Rua fainted right away. And when he came to, he was no more strong than you or I, for it was his magic finger that gave him all his strength.

So Oonagh sent Far Rua back to Scotland with a flea in his ear. And whenever anyone criticized Finn for his proud ways, Oonagh would tell them, "I know my husband, and he's got no more harm in him than a baby in a cradle!"

DUFFY AND THE DEVIL

I T WAS CIDER-MAKING time, and Squire Lovel of Trove rode up to Burian Church-town to ask for boys and girls to help bring in the apple harvest.

As he rode through the village, he heard a great shrieking and screaming coming from Janey Chygwin's cottage. As he arrived at the door, he saw the old woman beating her stepdaughter Duffy about the head with the skirt of her swing-tail gown, in which she had been carrying out the ashes. There was so much ash in the air that Squire Lovel nearly choked.

"What's going on?" he asked.

"It's Duffy, the lazy hussy!" said Janey. "She's always out with the boys, and will never stay in to boil the porridge, knit the stockings, or spin the yarn."

"Don't believe her, Squire Lovel," said Duffy. "My knitting and spinning is the best in the parish." And she ran her hand through her long black hair as she did so.

Squire Lovel liked the look of Duffy, so he said, "If you are so good at knitting and spinning, you shall come home with me. My old housekeeper is almost blind, and such work is beyond her now. Jump up behind me, Duffy."

So Duffy jumped up behind him and left her home without looking back.

When they got to the squire's house, the old half-blind housekeeper showed Duffy up to her room in the attic. It was piled from floor to ceiling with fleeces of wool. "If you'll just spin these for me, dear," said the old housekeeper, "that will be a start."

When Duffy was left alone, she sat down at the spinning wheel and cried. For truth to tell, Duffy was an idle girl and had never bothered to learn to knit or spin. She had never thought she would have to, being so pretty as she was, and having such wheedling ways.

"Curse this spinning and knitting," she said. "The devil may spin and knit for the squire for all I care!"

Scarcely had Duffy spoken these words when she heard a rustling noise behind the wool, and out walked an odd-looking little man, with strange eyes that seemed to flash with an inner light. He had a funny twist to his mouth, like someone who could see a joke that you couldn't. He was dressed all in black, and he stepped towards Duffy with a jaunty air, as if he were going to ask her for a dance.

"I'll be glad to do all the spinning and knitting for you, Duffy dear," he said.

"Thank you," said Duffy.

"I shall do the spinning, and you shall be a lady," he said.

"Thank you," said Duffy.

"But there's only one thing," said the little man. "If after three years you haven't found out my name, you must come away with me."

How hard could it be to find out a name? Duffy did not hesitate. "Thank you," she said. "I agree."

"In that case," said the little man, "you only have to wish, and any work you need to do shall be done."

So Duffy was able to spend her time lazing and lounging, and occasionally summoning up the energy to sing a song, and all she had to do was to wish that the fleeces had been spun into yarn, or that the yarn had been knitted into stockings, and it was done. Everyone said that they had never seen such fine work. Squire Lovel swore he would never wear stockings knitted by anyone else. He could wander all day through bushes and briars, through furze, and through brambles, and stay dry as a bone and never get a scratch.

So now Duffy could play the fine lady as much as she liked. Half of each day she lay in bed, and the other half she spent at the mill, where all the ladies of the parish would gather to tell stories or dance while their corn was being ground. When Duffy was there, the miller could usually be persuaded to saw away on his old fiddle, so that there was music for her to dance to. Sometimes the miller's wife, Old Bet, kept time by beating on sieve covered with sheepskin.

Now Old Bet was a witch, and she was the only one who noticed anything odd about the stockings Duffy knitted: there was always a stitch down. So Old Bet kept her eyes open, and soon she learned the secret of who did Duffy's work for her. But she did not tell anyone.

Duffy was now regarded as the best catch in the county, and young men came from all over to woo her; so the squire, who didn't want to lose someone who could knit such wonderful stockings, married her himself and made her Lady Lovel. But everyone still called her Duffy.

Duffy kept the little man hard at work. Stockings, fine underclothing, bedding, quilts, and even tapestries were produced at her command, and passed off as her own.

Duffy was as happy as could be, except she was never very comfortable about being high-and-mighty Lady Lovel. She spent more time with Old Bet at the mill than in her drawing room at Trove. And as for the squire, he didn't care about anyone or anything, as long as Duffy could keep him supplied with stockings, and he could go hunting every day.

The three years had nearly passed, and Duffy had tried every way to find out the devil's name, but she could not. Duffy fell into despair; for every day when she went up to the attic room, there he was, capering and cackling, and saying, "Soon you will be mine!"

When at last the gleeful little man said to her, "Tomorrow you will be mine!" Duffy did not know what to do.

Finally she confided in Old Bet, who said, "I have known all along that there would be a price to pay for the help of an imp such as that. But don't worry. If you let me help you, all will be well."

Old Bet told Duffy to bring her a barrel of strong beer from the cellar, and then to go home. She was not to go to bed before the squire came home, however late it was; nor was she to interrupt him, whatever he said.

When Duffy brought Old Bet the barrel of beer, she tucked it under her arm, along with the sieve she used to beat time for the dancing, wrapped her red cloak about her, and vanished into the night.

Duffy went home, and waited and waited for Squire Lovel to get back. By and by his dogs came home without him. They were covered in foam, and their tongues were hanging out of their mouths. The servants said that they must have met the devil's headless hounds.

It was after midnight when the squire finally arrived. Like a crazy, crack-brained man he kept singing:

> Here's to the devil,
> With his wooden pick and shovel.

He said, "Duffy, if you had seen what I have seen tonight, it would make you laugh to split your sides." And then he sang again:

> Here's to the devil,
> With his wooden pick and shovel.

At last he quieted down enough to tell her the story. "I had been hunting since dawn and never started a hare the livelong day. I was just coming home at nightfall when I saw Old Bet from the mill trudging past

81

the Pipers towards Dawnse Main. She seemed to vanish, and suddenly there was a hare, careering along, and the hounds after it. What a chase! On we went, through water and mud, until at last we came to a broad pool of water, and the hounds lost the scent. They ran back past me, howling and jowling, terrified to death."

Just as Old Bet had told her, Duffy did not say a word.

Squire Lovel continued, "I went on, and just round the corner I saw a glimmering fire, and gathering round the fire were all the witches of St. Leven. Some were riding on ragwort, some were riding on brooms, and those that had been to Wales to milk the cows were riding on great leeks. And chief amongst them all was Old Bet herself, with a sieve in her hand, and a barrel of my own best beer slung across her shoulders."

Still Duffy did not say a word.

"The witches all blew at the fire, and it burned up into a brilliant blue flame. And by that flame I could see an odd little man dressed in black, twirling his long forked tail. Bet struck her sieve and beat time as the witches all sang:

> Here's to the devil,
> With his wooden pick and shovel,
> Digging tin by the bushel,
> With his tail cocked up!

Then the devil and the witches began to dance round and round to the beat of the sieve, and each time the devil passed Old Bet he took a good swig of my beer."

Still Duffy did not say a word.

"At last the devil staggered and fell over. And he lay on the ground singing:

> Duffy, my lady, you'll never guess what,
> My name is Terrytop, Terrytop—top!"

Still Duffy did not say a word. She turned pale, and then red, and then pale again.

"Why aren't you laughing, Duffy? It was the funniest thing I ever saw in my life," said the squire.

And Duffy did laugh—the first true lighthearted laugh she had laughed for many's the day.

Next day, Duffy took care to wish for such an abundance of spinning and knitting that she would never want for any stockings or linen again. Then she went up to the attic, and the little man appeared.

"Well, Duffy my dear," he said. "I have served you faithfully for three years as we agreed, so now I hope you will go with me and make no objection." He bowed low, and his funny twisted grin broke into a broad smile.

"I'm worried that your country may be too hot for my complexion," said Duffy.

"It is not so hot as people say, Duffy," he replied. "Now come along. I have kept your word, and as you are a lady you must keep yours. Can you tell me my name? I'll give you three guesses."

"Is it Lucifer?"

He stamped his foot. "Lucifer! Lucifer! I wouldn't give him the time of day! Try again!"

"Is it perhaps Beelzebub?"

"Beelzebub! Beelzebub! A distant cousin of mine, no more. Try again." The little man was so full of glee that he danced around Duffy, whistling and cackling. He made as if to seize her by the waist and drag her down to hell.

"Stop! Stop! Stop!" shouted Duffy. "Your name is Terrytop!"

The little man looked at Duffy, and Duffy looked at him. "Deny it if you dare!" she said.

"I do not deny it," he said. "My name is Terrytop. It is not a name that is generally known on earth, and I did not expect a young minx like you, Duffy, to guess it. But you have beaten me, so I must take my leave."

And with that Duffy's devil vanished in a flash of fire and a puff of smoke, and she never saw him again.

MOLLY WHUPPIE

NCE UPON A time three sisters went out into the world to seek their fortune. The youngest of the three was called Molly Whuppie.

They walked and walked until nightfall. They began to shiver. They were alone in the dark without food or drink or shelter. So when they saw a light, they hurried to it.

Knock! Knock! at the door. A woman opened it an inch. "Go away," she said. "My man's a giant, and he'll eat you up."

"Please let us in," they begged, "and give us some bread and milk. We'll be gone before he comes home."

So she let them in and gave them bread and milk. But as soon as they began to eat, the earth shook, and the house trembled, and a voice rumbled:

> Snouk but and snouk ben,
> I smell the blood of some earthly one.

"Oh," said the wife, "it's only three lasses, cold and hungry, and they will go away. Let them be."

The giant sat down to his supper, and the table was groaning with food; he got up from his supper, and the table was bare. He wiped his beard and looked at Molly Whuppie and her sisters. "You can stay the night," he said, "and sleep with my own daughters."

So Molly Whuppie and her sisters lay down in the bed with the giant's three daughters. And when the giant tucked them up he tied a straw around Molly Whuppie's neck and around the necks of her sisters, and gold chains around the necks of his own three girls.

When everyone else was asleep, Molly slipped from the bed and took the gold chains off the giant's daughters and put them on herself and her sisters, and she took the straws off her sisters and put them on the giant's daughters, and then she lay down.

Soon the giant came back, fumbling across the room in the dark. He was carrying a great club. He put his hand on Molly's neck, felt the necklace of gold, and moved on. When he found the necklaces of straw, he took the three sleeping girls from the bed and hit them with his club until they shared not a spark of a breath between them. "They'll make a fine meat pie tomorrow," he muttered, and he went back to bed.

Molly thought it was time she and her sisters were out of there, so she woke them and put her finger to their lips. They stole silently out of the house, and ran and ran and never stopped until dawn. And when the sun came up they found they had come to a great palace.

In the palace was the king, and Molly told him how they had run away from the giant's house, and how she had tricked him into killing his own daughters instead of them.

The king said, "Molly, you're a clever girl, and you have managed well. But if you had brought me the giant's sword, which lies beside him every night, I would have given your first sister my first son to marry."

"Wait here," said Molly.

Back she went, into the giant's house, and hid under his bed.

She heard the giant come home, and the sound of his jaws as he ate his meal. And then she heard his footsteps coming up, up, up to the room where Molly was. She held her breath as the giant swung himself onto the bed.

When he was snoring, Molly crept out from under the bed and reached across him to take the sword. But as she took it, it gave a rattle, and up jumped the giant. Molly ran out of the door with the sword, and the giant ran after her.

She ran and she ran until they came to a river, and Molly plucked a hair from her head and made a bridge from it and crossed over; but the giant couldn't follow.

"A curse on you, Molly Whuppie," he cried. "Never come again."

"I'll come when my business brings me," she replied.

So Molly took the sword to the king, and her first sister was married to his first son.

The king said, "Molly, you're a clever girl, and you have managed well. But if you had brought me the purse that the giant keeps beneath his pillow, I would have given your second sister my second son to marry."

"Wait here," said Molly.

Back she went, into the giant's house, and hid under his bed.

She heard the giant come home, and the sound of his jaws as he ate his meal. And then she heard his footsteps coming up, up, up to the room where she was. She held her breath as the giant swung himself onto the bed.

When he was snoring, Molly crept out and slid her hand beneath his pillow to take the purse.

As she took it, it rattled and woke the giant. Molly ran out of the door with the purse, and the giant ran after her. She ran and she ran until they came to the one hair bridge, and she crossed; but the giant couldn't follow.

"A curse on you, Molly Whuppie," he cried. "Never come again."

"I'll come when my business brings me," she replied.

So Molly took the purse to the king, and her second sister was married to his second son.

The king said, "Molly, you're a clever girl, and you have managed well. But if you had brought me the ring from the giant's finger, I would have given you my third son for yourself."

"Wait here," said Molly.

Back she went, into the giant's house, and she hid under his bed.

She heard the giant come home, and the sound of his jaws as he ate his meal. And then she heard his footsteps coming up, up, up to the room where she was. She held her breath as the giant swung himself onto the bed.

When he was snoring, Molly crept out and caught hold of the giant's hand to take the ring from his finger.

As she slipped the ring off, it gave a rattle and woke the giant. Molly had hold of the ring; but the giant had hold of Molly.

"Now I have caught you, Molly Whuppie, tell me: If I had done to you what you have done to me, how would you get your revenge?"

"I would put you in a sack," said Molly, "and I would put the cat in with you, and the dog in with you, and a needle and thread and scissors, and I would hang you on the wall, and go to the wood, and cut the thickest stick I could find. Then I would come home and take you down and beat you until not a spark of a breath was left in you."

"Well Molly," said the giant, "that is just what I will do to you."

So he fetched a sack and put Molly in it, with the cat and the dog and a needle and thread and scissors, and hung her on the wall, and went off to the wood to choose a stick.

And Molly sang, "Oh, if you could see what I can see!"

"What do you see, Molly?" asked the giant's wife.

But Molly never answered. She just sang again, "Oh, if you could see what I can see!"

"Let me look, Molly, let me look," pleaded the giant's wife. "I want to see it too."

So Molly took the scissors and cut a hole in the sack and jumped down with the needle and thread. She helped the giant's wife into the sack and sewed up the hole.

"It's very dark in here," said the giant's wife. "I can't see anything." But Molly wouldn't let her out.

Molly hid behind the door. The giant came in with a great tree in his hand. He took down the sack and started hitting it. His wife yelled out, "It's me!" but what with the barking of the dog and the mewing of the cat, the giant didn't recognize his own wife's voice in all the racket.

Molly came out from behind the door, with the ring in her hand. "You can't catch me," she shouted, and she ran off with the ring. The giant left off beating the sack and ran after her.

Molly ran and ran until she came to the one hair bridge, and she crossed; but the giant couldn't follow.

"A curse on you, Molly Whuppie," he cried. "Never come again."

"I've no more business to bring me," she replied.

So Molly took the ring to the king, and she was married to his third son, and she never tangled with the giant again.

THE BLACK CAT

HERE WAS ONCE a widower who married a widow. They each already had a child from their previous marriages, two girls of roughly the same age. The man's was called Yvonne, and was as sweet, kind, and pretty as the other, who was called Louise, was ugly, selfish, and spiteful. But the woman did not like Yvonne, and always took the side of her own daughter.

When the girls were sixteen or seventeen, young men began to call on them. The mother always made sure her own daughter, Louise, was looking her best in a new dress, while Yvonne was left in cast-off rags. But despite that, the young men only had eyes for Yvonne.

The mother understood that if Louise was to shine, Yvonne had to be got out of the way. So she sent her off to the wide moor each day to look after a little black cow, with orders not to return before sunset. All she had to eat all day was a hunk of black bread and a dry biscuit.

Because she was alone all day with only the black cow and her little dog, Faithful, Yvonne became very fond of the cow and thought of it as her best friend. She told it all her secrets and called it Little Golden Heart.

The cow, which had been thin and puny, grew sleek and plump in Yvonne's care. When the mother noticed this, and saw how much Yvonne loved the cow, she said, "That cow has been fattened up very nicely. We should slaughter it, and give a feast for my Louise's birthday."

So the cow was killed, and Yvonne suffered a great sadness.

When the cow was cut open, they found a pair of little golden slippers next to the heart. The mother took them, saying, "Louise can wear these at her wedding."

Some days later, a very rich prince, who had heard tell of the beauty and gentle nature of Yvonne, came to see her. The scheming mother told Yvonne to put on Louise's fine clothes and jewels, and presented her to the prince. Yvonne charmed him, and he lost no time in asking her to marry him. Yvonne said yes, and the marriage day was set then and there. Then the prince went back to his kingdom, promising to return for the wedding.

But when the day arrived, the mother made sure that the bride was not Yvonne but but her own daughter. It was Louise who was dressed in the bridal gown, with her face covered by a veil, and the golden slippers on her feet. The slippers were too small for her, but her mother had solved that by chopping off her heels and toes to fit. Meanwhile poor Yvonne was locked up in a tower.

The prince was so dazzled by all her gold and diamonds that he didn't notice the deception and got in the gilded coach with his bride to be. Poor little Faithful, Yvonne's dog, ran after the coach, yapping:

> Beware of sullen ugly-nose
> With clipped heels and shorn toes!
> Alas! Alas! The pretty one
> Is left locked up to weep and moan!

But nobody heard or understood.

When they got to the church door, the false bride tried to step down from the carriage. But she could scarcely walk in the golden slippers. As she stumbled along, she couldn't help groaning with pain. The prince went to help her, and it was then that he saw that this was not the girl with whom he had fallen in love.

"I have been tricked!" he said. "You are not the girl I met. Get out of my sight!"

The prince went back to his kingdom in a fury, and the mother and Louise set out for home. Both were weeping hot tears of anger and frustration. Louise had so nearly been married to a prince! It was all Yvonne's fault, they told each other, and they swore a terrible revenge.

On the way home, they called in at a cottage in a wood where an old witch lived. The witch told them to go back to the house and to kill a black cat which lived there, cook it, and serve it to Yvonne as jugged hare. "She will think it a special treat, and will go to sleep happy, but she will never wake up again. In the morning you will find her dead in her bed."

So when they got back, the mother herself caught the cat, killed it, skinned it, prepared it as jugged hare, and served it to Yvonne.

Poor Yvonne, who never thought badly of anyone, truly believed that her stepmother was trying to make amends for locking her in the tower, and ate every scrap.

After supper, the mother wished Yvonne goodnight. "Sleep well," she said.

But soon after, Yvonne began to feel ill. She was terribly sick, and threw up everything she had eaten. It must have been that that saved her.

Next morning, when the mother looked in on Yvonne, she was astonished to find her still alive. "Did you have a good night?" she asked.

"Oh! Mother!" said Yvonne. "I've been very ill. I almost died last night."

"Nonsense," said the mother. "You just had a bilious attack. Let it teach you not to be so greedy."

94

The mother went back to the witch to ask what to do. The witch told her, "You must make life so miserable for Yvonne and her father that they decide to leave of their own accord."

The mother followed the witch's advice. She nagged and criticized her husband until he thought he would go mad, and she ill-treated Yvonne until she wanted to die.

So the father and daughter made plans to leave. They got hold of a small boat, and one night in secret they went down to the shore to sail away. But the mother, who had been waiting and watching, ran after them and told her husband, "Stop, you fool! You can't leave without your red book! You know you would be lost without it!" And the poor man was so used to obeying his wife that he turned round and went back to the house to fetch his red book.

No sooner was he out of sight than the wicked woman untied the boat. The brisk land breeze carried it far out to sea, until Yvonne's cries for help could no longer be heard.

Now Yvonne was very frightened, all alone at the mercy of the tides and the winds. But as luck would have it the boat came safely to shore at last on a small island. Yvonne explored the whole island, hoping to find a house, but it was deserted. However, she did find a cave, which even contained a bed and a cooking pot. "A hermit must live here," she told herself. But no one came back to the cave. At last Yvonne gathered some shellfish to eat and lay down to sleep.

When she awoke, she heard a faint mewing. And at the bottom of the bed, she found a little black kitten.

She looked after the kitten and loved him as much as if her were her own child. She played with him and took him with her when she gathered shellfish along the seashore or picked fruit on the island.

The kitten grew fast, and after two or three months it was a splendid cat, such as you rarely see.

One day when Yvonne was talking to the black cat, telling him all her troubles much as she used to talk to the little black cow, she said, "You look so intelligent. I'm sure you understand every word I say."

And the cat answered, "I do."

Yvonne was amazed. "How is it you can talk like a man?" she asked.

"I can't tell you now, Mother," said the cat. "A time will come when all your sufferings are at an end, and then you will know. In the meantime, make me a knapsack I can wear on my back, and I will swim to the mainland and fetch you something better to eat than raw shellfish."

Yvonne did not want to let the cat swim so far, but he insisted, saying, "As I am doing it for love of you, I can come to no harm." So she made him a knapsack, and he plunged into the sea. Yvonne watched him swimming until he disappeared from view.

When the cat reached land he found himself in a fine sea port—it might have been Lannion, or perhaps Treguier—and set out to find some provisions. Schoolboys on the quayside laughed at him, prowling along with his knapsack like a beggar, and threw stones at him, so he ducked inside the nearest house. It belonged to Mr. Rio, the richest man in town. He had once been a prince, but he had given up his kingdom, because he had been disappointed in love.

The cat went to the kitchen door, and called, *Meow! Meow!* The cook went to the door with her broom to chase the strange black cat away and was amazed when he coolly asked, "Is Mr. Rio at home?"

"No," said the cook. "But he will be back later."

"I'm afraid I haven't time to wait," replied the cat. "I wonder if you would be so kind as to fill this knapsack with food for me."

"No I would not," said the cook.

So the cat went to the spit where a chicken was roasting for Mr. Rio's

dinner and took it himself, along with a good slice of bacon, a loaf of white bread, and a bottle of fine wine. He put them in his knapsack, slung it back over his shoulders, and with a cheery "Good-bye" slipped out of the house.

He made his way back to the shore along the tops of walls and underneath hedges, to avoid the schoolboys, and then he swam back to the island.

"Look, Mother," he said, opening his knapsack. "This should make a better meal than you are used to. And there is plenty more where it came from." So they set to and ate their fill.

Meanwhile, when Mr. Rio got home and saw there was nothing to eat, he asked the cook sharply, "Where's my dinner."

"Oh! Mr. Rio!" said the flustered cook. "A big black cat came, with a knapsack on his shoulder, and took it all!"

"You can't expect me to believe a fairy tale like that," he said. But the cook insisted it was true.

A few days later, when all the provisions were gone, the cat swam back to the port and went once again to Mr. Rio's kitchen door. *Meow! Meow!*

This time, Mr. Rio was at home. He came down from his room with a loaded gun in his hand. The cat wasn't scared of that.

"What do you want?" asked Rio.

"The same as before: meat, bread, and wine for my mother and myself."

Rio gave him the food, and the cat thanked him.

"Now I'll give you some advice," the cat said. "I know that you are in love with a girl, and think she is going to marry you. You have even left her all your money in your will. But she has another lover, and they are planning to kill you. Soon you are going on a hunting party, and you will be asked to share a room with your rival. He will go to sleep next to the wall, and you will be on the outside. When he is asleep, you must be sure to roll him over and change places with him. For in the night your false love will creep into the room, with a big knife which she will have whetted to a razor edge that very day, and cut the neck of the sleeper on the outside, thinking it is you. So be warned. Do exactly as I say, or it will be the worse for you. And whatever happens, trust me. I will come to your aid, at the right time."

Now Rio did not know what to think. When an invitation came asking him to a hunting party, he thought of refusing. But then he would never know if the cat had spoken the truth. So he went, and everything happened exactly as the black cat had foretold.

Rio remembered the cat's advice, and when his rival was fast asleep, he changed places. Then he put out the light, and pretended to be sound asleep too. Soon after, he heard a creak as the door was slowly opened, and the tiptoe of his false love's feet as she crossed the floor. She had a great hunting knife in her hand, and she used it to cut the throat of the sleeping man. Then she left and locked the door behind her.

There was nothing Rio could do. He was locked in with no chance of escape.

In the morning, when neither Rio nor the other man came down for breakfast, their wicked hostess said, "Let's go and wake them." She led the way to their room, deftly unlocked the door, and flung it open. When she saw that she had killed the wrong man she shrieked in grief and anger. Before Rio could say a thing, she cried, "This evil man has killed his night's companion! Tie him up and throw him in jail! He shall hang for this."

Everyone agreed that Rio had murdered the man and deserved to die. So a scaffold was built, and the next morning Rio was taken to it to be hung. The murderess watched it all from her balcony, with all her friends.

Rio looked at her in despair. And then he saw, on the roof, the black cat. He said, "I have no more hope in mankind, but if that black cat up there on the roof could speak the truth, I know I would be saved."

All eyes turned to the cat. It sprang down to the scaffold next to Rio and spoke to the headsman. "Hold it! This man is innocent. It was not he who killed his companion, but that wicked woman over there." And he pointed at the woman on the balcony, who gave a cry and fainted right away.

When she came to, the woman was so frightened of the talking cat who seemed to know all her secrets that she admitted her crime. So Mr. Rio was pardoned, and she was beheaded in his place.

Then Rio returned home, and the cat went back to the island.

Some days later, the cat said to Yvonne, "Mother, it is time you got married."

"Who could I marry?" she asked.

"I know just the man," said the cat. "Trust me, and I will arrange it all."

The cat swam back to the port and went to Mr. Rio's house.

Rio was very pleased to see him. "I can't thank you enough," he said. "I wish there were something I could do for you."

"There is," said the cat. "I want you to marry my mother."

"I know I owe you my life," said Rio. "But you can't expect me to marry a cat."

"Believe me, Mr. Rio, my mother is worthy of you. Marry her, and you won't regret it."

"Perhaps when I've seen her ... then we'll see," said Rio.

"I'll bring her tomorrow," said the cat.

With that the cat departed. Rio was in a terrible fix. He didn't want to upset the cat and seem ungrateful, but he didn't want to marry a cat either.

After leaving Rio's house, the cat slipped in the window of a rich lady's house and filled his knapsack with silk and velvet dresses and fine jewels for Yvonne to wear. He used one of the diamonds to pay a ferryman to take him to the island to fetch her.

Now Yvonne was still as lovely as ever, and when she had put on the fine clothes and jewels that the cat had fetched her she was a dazzling beauty. Mr. Rio fell in love with her at first sight—for she was the very girl he had tried to marry, when he had been a prince.

The black cat asked, "Now, Mr. Rio, would you like to marry my mother?"

"With all my heart," he replied.

They were married next week, with much feasting and celebration.

After the wedding, the black cat said, "Now we must take your new husband and introduce him to your father, and your stepmother, and your sister Louise." So they got into a coach and set off for Yvonne's old home.

When they arrived, her father was overjoyed to see his daughter again, and so was little Faithful. The stepmother and her daughter, who was still unmarried, were full of spite and jealousy, but they pretended to be pleased to see her. They even arranged a feast to welcome her home; but they asked the old witch as one of the guests, hoping she would come up with another plan to get rid of Yvonne for good.

Halfway through the meal the witch turned pale and tried to leave, saying she felt poorly. She had felt something brush against her leg, and when she looked down, it was the black cat.

Then the black cat leaped up on the table, his back arched, his tail bushed out, and his eyes flaring. "Stop her!" he shouted.

Everyone was frightened and astonished, except for Mr. Rio and Yvonne.

The servants brought the old witch back to the table, struggling and protesting.

"Silence, you old snake," said the cat. "Judgment day has come for you. You must fight me, by water, wind, or fire."

The witch said, "I am not afraid of you, by water, wind, or fire."

"Then let us start with water," said the cat.

They went into the courtyard and prepared to fight. Everyone was watching from the windows.

First the old witch began to spit water at the cat. The water came out of her mouth like a wave, to drown him. But for every barrelful the witch spat out, the cat spat three. So she was forced to beg for mercy.

Then the old witch began to blow. A roaring wind came from her mouth to blow the cat away. But he blew back, and his breath was so much stronger that it lifted her up like a straw and pinned her to the wall. So she was forced to beg for mercy again.

"Now it is the turn of fire!" said the cat.

They began to spit fire at each other, like two angry dragons, or two devils from hell.

But the old witch's flames died out, and the cat's overwhelmed her and burned her to ash.

The cat went back into the dining hall. "One has paid the price," he said, "but there is still another."

The stepmother was white and trembling. She felt her hour had come. The cat said, "Yes, madam, it is your turn now."

"But what have I done to you?" she asked.

"Remember the jugged hare?" said the cat. And then he spat fire again and burned her to a cinder.

Then he turned to Louise, who was pale and glassy-eyed. "As for you, my girl, I won't do you any harm. You were too young to understand your mother's evil plans. The guilt was hers, not yours."

He said to Faithful, the little dog, "It is your duty to look after Louise, and show her how to love."

And lastly he turned to Rio. "Now, Mr. Rio, put me on my back on the table, and slit me open with your sword."

"I can't do that," said Rio.

"Do as I tell you. You owe me that," said the cat.

So Rio took the black cat, stretched him on his back on the table, and slit his stomach open with his sword.

And out stepped a handsome man, who said, "I am the greatest magician who ever lived on earth!"

After that, the merrymaking went on for eight days, and the man who had been the black cat sang and danced and told stories and did tricks the whole time.

THE KING AND THE WORKMAN'S DAUGHTER

 NE DAY, A workman was digging a drain when the king stopped by and asked him what he was doing.

"I am working," said the workman.

"Does it pay?" asked the king.

"Sometimes it does and sometimes it doesn't," said the workman. "It depends on the ground."

"Are you married?" asked the king.

"I was, but now I am a widower."

"And do you have any children?"

"Just the one daughter."

"And how old is she?"

"She is twelve years old."

Then the workman started back digging his drain. The king said, "Just one more question . . ." but the workman said, "Don't bother me with any more fool questions."

"I will ask you another question," said the king, "and if you can't answer it by twelve o'clock tomorrow, you will be hanged. The question is: How long would it take me to travel around the world?"

"How should I know that?" said the workman.

"You must find out, if you don't want to be hanged," said the king. "Now I am going home, but I will return tomorrow at twelve for your answer."

When the workman got home that night, he was very sad. His

daughter, seeing that he was not his usual self, asked, "Father, is something wrong?"

"The king came today and asked me a question no one could solve. Yet if I do not solve it, I will be hanged."

"What is it?"

"He asked me how long it would take him to travel around the world."

"That's not so hard," said the workman's daughter. "You have your supper and get a good night's rest, and in the morning I will tell you how to answer the king."

And the next morning, good as her word, the workman's daughter told him how to answer the king's question. So when the king came by at twelve o'clock, expecting to find the workman in fear and trembling, instead he heard him whistling as he worked.

"Have you solved the question?" asked the king.

"I have tried," said the workman.

"And what is your answer?"

"Your Majesty could go around the world in twenty-four hours," said the workman.

"How do you make that out?" asked the king.

And the workman said, as his daughter had told him, "All you have to do is put a saddle on the sun, and you can ride right around the world in twenty-four hours."

The king thought for a moment, looked down at the ground and up at the sun, and burst out laughing. "Very good," he said. "Powerful as I am, even I cannot saddle the sun. But I wager that you did not think of that answer yourself. Who told you what to say?"

"As I answered the question, it's no business of yours who told me what to say," answered the workman.

"In that case," said the king, "I will ask you another question, and if you cannot answer this one by twelve o'clock tomorrow, you will be hanged. The question is: What is the distance between the earth and the sky?"

When the workman got home that night, he was just as sad as before.

"Did the king not like my answer to his question?" asked the workman's daughter.

"He did," said the workman, "but now he has asked me an even harder question, and if I cannot answer it, I must be hanged. He wants to know the distance between the earth and the sky."

"That's not so hard," said the workman's daughter. "You eat your supper and get a good night's rest, and in the morning I will tell you what to do."

That morning, after his daughter had told him what to do, the workman set off early for the king's palace. He stood on the lawn, took off his coat, and hammered two wooden pins into the ground.

The king opened his bedroom window and looked out. "What do you think you're doing," he shouted angrily.

"With your permission," replied the workman, "I am going to measure the distance between the earth and the sky. All I need now is a line that will stretch all the way. As you are king, I am sure you have enough gold and silver to buy me one."

The king thought for a moment. He looked down at the workman, and up at the sky, and then he burst out laughing. "Very good," he said. "Rich as I am, even I cannot buy such a line. But I wager that you did not think of that yourself. Who put you up to it?"

"I solved it myself," said the workman.

"No you did not," said the king. "If you do not tell me who solved it, I will have you hanged."

So the frightened workman told him, "It was my daughter who solved your questions."

"How old is she?"

"Twelve years old."

"In that case, she can come and live in the palace," said the king.

"But who will look after my house, and cook my food, and do my washing?" asked the workman.

"Don't worry about that," said the king. "Let her come to me, and I will be a good friend to you. She is a girl with a head on her shoulders, so she should live in the palace."

The workman brought his daughter to the king, and she began work in the palace, scouring knives and polishing candlesticks. As the years passed, she grew into a tall and elegant young woman, but all the other servants still looked down on her, and sneered at her, and would never call her anything but "the workman's daughter." So when she came of age she told the king that she wanted to leave his palace.

"Why?" asked the king.

"Because the other servants look down on me, and call me 'the workman's daughter,'" she said.

"That is easily solved," he answered. "I will make your father a knight, and then they will have to call you 'the knight's daughter.'"

And so she stayed at the palace and was promoted to wait at the king's table.

She was so graceful and lovely that the king fell in love with her and asked her to marry him.

"That cannot be," she said, "for you must marry a princess, and I should marry a man I choose for myself."

"But it must be," said the king, "for I cannot live without you."

"If it must be, it shall be," she said.

"I have only one thing to say," said the king. "You must never contradict my royal judgment. If you do, you shall be turned out of the palace to fend for yourself."

"I agree, on one condition," she answered. "If I am ever turned out of the palace, I must be allowed to take with me any three armfuls that I wish. And I would like that in writing."

"You will get it," said the king.

So they were married, and the workman's daughter became a queen. Within a year she had given birth a fine young prince. Everything was perfect.

Now it happened that near the palace lived two men who were bitter enemies. One of them had a mare and its foal, and the other had a white stallion. The foal had got into the habit of following the white stallion across the fields, and one day it followed the stallion all the way home. Then the stallion's owner shut it in his paddock and refused to give it back.

The mare's owner went to the king and complained, but the stallion's owner said the foal was his.

The king said, "As you both claim the foal, both of you should put your horses in the paddock with the foal, then leave the gate open. The foal belongs with whichever horse it follows."

The foal followed the white stallion, so the king ruled that it belonged to the stallion's owner.

The owner of the mare went to the queen and told her how he had been robbed of his foal.

"I see that you have been wronged," she said, "but I cannot contradict the king's royal judgment. If I do so, I shall cease to be queen. However, I can tell you what to do. Get a small basketful of peas. Boil the peas and put them back in the basket. Then take them into the field and, when you see the king coming, sow them in the ground." And the queen told the man everything he should do and say.

Next time the king rode by the man's farm, he found him sowing the

boiled peas. "You fool," said the king, "do you think that they will grow?"

"It is just as likely," said the man, "as that a stallion should give birth to a foal."

The king thought for a moment. He looked at the man, and he looked at the peas. "Very good," he said. "Clever as I am, even I can make a mistake. But you did not think of that for yourself."

The king went home in a blinding rage. He caught the queen roughly by the shoulder and said, "You shall be turned out of the palace today."

"Why?" she asked.

"Because you have contradicted my royal judgment in the case of the man who had the foal."

"Very well," she said, "but remember, I am entitled to three armfuls of my choice." And she produced the paper that he had signed.

"Yes, yes, yes," he said.

"Now," she said, "put on your royal robe, so that I may bid you good-bye."

The king put on his robe.

"Now, sit in your royal chair."

The king sat down.

The queen then put her arms around both him and the chair and lifted them out through the door.

"That is my first armful," she said.

Then she went back inside and fetched the baby prince, and put him in the king's lap.

"That is my second armful," she said.

Then she went back inside and fetched all the royal charters and seals, and put them in the prince's lap.

"That is everything," she said. "We can go now."

And the king said, "You are the dearest and wisest of women, and I am a foolish man. From now on, nothing but death can separate us!" He led her back into the palace, and his first act was to send a servant, in the name of the queen, to order the man with the horse to give the foal back to its rightful owner.

And from then on, the king asked the queen's opinion before he made any decisions about anything.

THE SOUL CAGES

N THE EAST coast of County Clare lived a man called Jack Dogherty. He was a fisherman, as his father and grandfather had been before him.

He lived in a lonely house right on the coast, where he could look out across the ocean and see before anyone else when a boat was being wrecked on the treacherous rocks beneath the waves. And then Jack would set out in his little boat to aid poor souls in trouble, and to help himself to any bales of cotton or kegs of rum or suchlike that spilled from the wreck.

Now Jack had one dear wish, and that was to see a merrow, one of the sea-people, for he had often heard of them but had never seen one save as a shadow beneath the waves. It was said that his grandfather had even had one as a friend.

At last one day he spied in the distance something perched on a rock in the sea. It was green and indistinct, but he could have sworn that it was holding a cocked hat in its hand. He stood for half an hour staring at it, but it never moved. Then, just as he began to think he was imagining things, it dived from the rock into the sea.

After that, Jack kept a close eye on that rock. One rough day, when the sea was running mountains high, he saw the green merrow again. It was diving from the rock into the pounding waves, then climbing back up and diving in again. So Jack understood that if he wanted to see the merrow, he should keep a lookout on stormy days.

On one such day, when the wind was blustering and howling, the storm came on so strongly and suddenly that Jack had to take refuge in a cave. And there, to his astonishment, he found the merrow. It had green hair, long green teeth, a red nose, and pig's eyes. It had a fish's tail, legs with scales on them, and short arms like fins. It had no clothes, but held a cocked hat under its arm and looked very solemn and thoughtful.

Jack made a bow. "Your servant, sir," he said.

"Your servant, Jack Dogherty," replied the merrow.

"How do you know my name?" cried Jack in astonishment.

"You're the spitting image of your grandfather," said the merrow, "and he was a great friend of mine. Many's the time he came with me to my house to drink a shellful of brandy. And you would be as welcome as he was."

"I can't see how that could be," said Jack.

"Meet me here on Monday," said the merrow, "and I will show you."

When Jack went back to the cave on Monday, the merrow was there again, and this time he was holding two cocked hats.

"I want you to put on this hat," said the merrow, "and dive down to my house beneath the sea."

"How can I do that?" asked Jack. "I should be drowned for sure."

"Many's the time your grandfather put on that hat and swam down with me. Are you not the man your grandfather was?"

So they swam out to the rock and climbed up onto it, and then the merrow gave Jack the hat to put on. "Follow me," the merrow cried, and he dived off the far side, into the deep dark sea.

Jack was frightened, but he thought, *If my grandfather did it, I can do it too.* So he dived after the merrow.

Down and down they went, with Jack holding onto the merrow's fish tail. At last they came out under the water, to a neat little house roofed with oyster shells. Above it, the sea arched like the sky does over the land, and in it fishes were swimming about like birds.

"Now," said the merrow, "let's see what's for supper."

They went inside. In the kitchen, two young merrows were cooking a meal. Jack lifted the lid off the pot, and it smelled wonderful.

Then the merrow led him through to the cellar, which was stacked floor to ceiling with barrels and kegs of brandy and rum that had come from the same shipwrecks that provided Jack with his livelihood.

Then they went back into the snug kitchen and dined like kings.

At the end of the meal, Jack lifted his shell of brandy in a toast. "Here's to your health," he said, "although I don't know your name."

"My name is Coomara," said the merrow, "and here's to your health, too."

"May you live another fifty years, Coomara," wished Jack.

"Make it five hundred, Jack," said Coomara.

And so, toasting one another and wishing each other health and long life, Coomara and Jack emptied shell after shell of brandy, and soon they fell to singing. Coomara taught Jack one of the merrows' songs, and this is how the chorus goes:

> *Rum fum boodle boo,*
> *Ripple dipple nitty dob;*
> *Dumdoo doodle coo,*
> *Raffle taffle chittibob!*

But if you want to know what it means, you'll have to dive down beneath the sea and ask the merrows, for no one on earth knows.

At last, Coomara said, "Now I will show you my collection of curiosities." He led Jack into a large room full of odds and ends. The most striking thing about the room was that one wall was filled with what looked like lobster pots.

"What are those?" asked Jack.

"Oh! Those are the soul cages," said Coomara.

"The what?"

"The soul cages. You know, for keeping souls in."

"Souls! Do fish have souls then?" asked Jack.

"Not fish, sailors! When a storm is brewing, I set my cages beneath the sea, and when the souls leave the bodies of the drowning sailors, they take refuge in my pots, and then I take them home."

And then it was time to go. Coomara made Jack put the hat on backwards, and dive up through the sea. He shot up like a bubble, and soon he was back on the shore. Then he threw the hat back into the sea, where it sunk like a stone.

Now Jack was a lighthearted, easygoing kind of man, not given to worrying. But he couldn't get the thought of the poor souls in the soul cages out of his head. At last, he hit on a plan.

Next time they met in the cave, Jack asked Coomara to come and dine with him. Then he said, "I know you have drunk the finest brandy and the rarest rum, but I'll wager you have never had a drop of the real mountain dew."

"What is that?" asked Coomara.

"Why, poteen," said Jack. "You make it from potatoes, and it is the finest drink of all."

So Coomara had one glass of poteen, and then another, and then another. Soon he was singing *"Rum fum boodle boo,"* and soon after that he collapsed on the floor fast asleep. For poteen is stronger than any other drink, and Coomara had no head for it.

As soon as Coomara was snoring, Jack seized the cocked hat and went down to the sea. He dived off the rock, and soon arrived at Coomara's house. There, he went into the storeroom, and opened all the soul cages. He could not see anything, for no man can see the soul any

more than he can see the wind, but he thought he heard a sort of whistle or chirp as he opened each cage.

When the last soul cage was opened, Jack put the hat on backwards and set off for home.

There he found Coomara just waking up, and complaining of a terrible headache.

"Oh, that's nothing," said Jack. "Another glass of poteen will cure it."

But Coomara said he had had quite enough, thank you, and with that he put on his cocked hat and went back to his home beneath the sea. And the merrow never knew who had freed the souls from his soul cages, and nor did he ever touch a drop of poteen again so long as he lived.

THE FIDDLER IN THE CAVE

I N NORTH WALES there is cave on a hillside which no one dares go near, for it is a fairy place. Once, when the hunt drove a fox to the mouth of the cave, the poor hunted creature turned round with his hair standing on end and ran into the middle of the pack rather than enter it.

One Halloween, the fiddler Iolo ap Hugh was listening to a shepherd's stories of the dangers of the cave and said, "I am not afraid to enter any cave in this world." And to prove it, he packed bread and cheese and candles into a knapsack, tucked his fiddle under his arm, and went to the cave to see what he should see.

His friends waited for him at the inn all that night, but he never returned.

Just once, many years later, the shepherd passed by the mouth of the cave on the night of Halloween, searching for a lost sheep. From inside the cave came the sound of a fiddle—not the lilting melody of a country dance, but the jolting wails of a soul in torment.

The shepherd peered into the darkness of the cave, and there, in the glimmering half-light of a candle, he saw Iolo ap Hugh, dancing to the groans and sighs of his own fiddle. His face was as pale as marble, and his eyes were blank and staring. His hand sawed the bow over the fiddle, and his feet jerked and capered like a mechanical doll.

Iolo's steps took him to the very brink of the cave and then dragged him back again, like the smoke up a chimney, until he disappeared from

119

view, leaving only the broken echo of his fiddle ringing in the shepherd's ears.

More years passed, and Iolo ap Hugh was given up as lost.

Then, one Sunday, the old shepherd was sitting in church with the other parishioners, when a shiver suddenly ran through them all. A burst of music, passionate and wild, rose from beneath the floor and filled the church, then died away till it could not be distinguished from the wailing of the wind.

The shepherd recognized the music. It was the same tune that he had heard when he saw Iolo ap Hugh fiddling and dancing in the mouth of the cave.

The tune was written down from the old shepherd's whistling, and it is famous in Wales to this day, under the name "Farewell Ned Pugh." It is said that if you were to go to that cave on the night of Halloween, and listen at the cave mouth, you would hear that tune, as distinctly as you hear the waves roaring in a seashell.

THE WELL AT THE WORLD'S END

HERE WAS A king and a queen, and the king had a daughter and the queen had a daughter. And the king's daughter was bonny and good-natured, and everybody liked her; and the queen's daughter was ugly and ill-natured, and nobody liked her.

The queen hated the king's daughter and wanted to get rid of her. So she sent her to the well at the world's end to get a bottle of water, thinking she would never come back.

The king's daughter took a bottle and she walked and walked until she came to a pony that was tethered to a bush, and the pony said:

> Free me, free me, my bonny May,
> For I haven't been free for seven years and a day.

And the king's daughter said, "I will, my bonny pony." So she untied the pony, and it gave her a ride over the moor of hecklepins.

Well, she went far and far and farther than I can tell, till she came to the well at the world's end. When she came to the well it was very deep, and she could not dip her bottle into the water. So she looked down into the well, wondering what to do, and saw three men's heads looking up at her. They said to her:

> Wash me, wash me, my bonny May,
> And dry me with your clean linen apron.

And she said, "I will." So she washed the three heads, and dried them with the clean linen apron, and they took her bottle and dipped it in the water for her.

And then the heads said, one to the other:

> Weird, brother, weird, what'll you weird?

And the first one said, "I weird that if she was bonny before, she'll be ten times bonnier." And the second one said, "I weird that each time she speaks, a diamond, a ruby, and a pearl will drop from her mouth." And the third one said, "I weird that each time she combs her hair, she'll get a peck of gold and a peck of silver out of it."

Well, she went home to the king's court, and if she was bonny before, now she was ten times bonnier; and every time she spoke, a diamond, a ruby, and a pearl dropped from her mouth; and every time she combed her hair, she got a peck of gold and a peck of silver out of it.

The queen was so angry she didn't know what to do with herself. But at last she thought she would send her own daughter to see if she would have the same luck. So she gave her a bottle and told her to go to the well at the world's end and get a bottle of water.

The queen's daughter walked and walked until she came to the pony, and the pony said:

> Free me, free me, my bonny May,
> For I haven't been free for seven years and a day.

And the queen's daughter said, "Why should I free you, you nasty beast. Don't you know who you're speaking to? I'm a queen's daughter."

So she didn't free the pony, and the pony didn't give her a ride over the moor of hecklepins, so the thorns cut her bare feet, and by the time she reached the well at the world's end she could hardly walk.

She looked down into the well, and the three heads said to her:

> Wash me, wash me, my bonny May,
> And dry me with your clean linen apron.

And she said, "You dirty, nasty things, why should I wash you? Don't you know who you're speaking to? I'm a queen's daughter."

So she didn't wash the heads, and they wouldn't dip her bottle for her.

And the three heads said one to the other:

Weird, brother, weird, what'll you weird?

And the first one said, "I weird that if she was ugly before, she'll be ten times uglier." And the second said, "I weird that each time she speaks, a toad and a frog will jump out of her mouth." And the third said, "I weird that each time she combs her hair, she'll get a peck of lice and a peck of fleas out of it."

So she went home again, and if she was ugly before, now she was ten times uglier; and each time she spoke, a toad and a frog jumped out of her mouth; and each time she combed her hair, she got a peck of lice and a peck of fleas out of it.

So they had to send her away from court. And a handsome young prince came and married the king's daughter; but the queen's daughter had to put up with an old cobbler, and he beat her each day with a leather strap.

THE SHIP THAT WENT TO AMERICA

THIS SHIP SAILED to America, carrying a great number of people who were emigrating. But when they neared land, the ship was wrecked on the rocks, and all were lost except one man and his wife.

These two drifted ashore clinging to a piece of wood, and using sails and ropes from the wreck they managed to rig up a tent on the shore and feed themselves with provisions from the ship. But this food and drink was soon nearly gone.

The man told his wife not to worry. "I will go inland and see if I can find any houses or men." He set off, and soon came into a huge wood. As he walked, he marked the bark of the trees so that he would be able to find his way back. At last he came out the other side, but he still could not see any houses. There was a mountain in the distance, so he decided to climb it and see what he could see from the top.

By the time he had climbed the mountain the day was nearly gone. He was tired and hungry, and beginning to wish he had never left his tent. But then he looked down from the mountain top and spied a little hut at the foot of the mountain. So he set off to investigate.

When he reached the hut, he went in and found a table covered with a large white tablecloth, on which were set a bottle of wine and a loaf of bread. "Well," he said to himself. "I am hungry and thirsty. Surely no one would begrudge me some bread and wine." So he poured himself a glass of wine and cut himself a slice of bread.

As he did so, a white-haired old man came in, asking, "What's your news, stranger? What wind has driven you in this direction?"

The man explained about the shipwreck. "I hope you don't mind my helping myself to bread and wine. I was hungry."

"Not at all, not at all," said the white-haired old man. "Help yourself. It is there for people such as you. Are you married?"

"I am. I have left my wife in a tent on the shore."

"And do you have any children?"

"No. We never had any children."

"It is too late to return to your wife tonight; the day is over. Stay here tonight, and I will give you food and shelter."

In the morning, there was another bottle of wine and another loaf on the table, and the man made a good breakfast. Then he said good-bye to the white-haired old man.

His host said, "Before you leave, tell me, how much would you give me for this tablecloth? Every time that you spread it on your table you will get a bottle of wine and a loaf of bread."

"I would give much for it," said the man, "but really, I have nothing to give."

"Well," said the old man, "if you will promise to give me the first man or beast that is born on your property, I shall give you the cloth as a present."

As the man thought that he and his wife would never have any children, nor ever own any animals, he agreed. So the old man gave him the tablecloth, saying, "Whatever it is that is born first, bring it to me here seven years from today."

So the man walked back to his wife with the magic tablecloth, and they lived happily in the tent on the shore on bread and wine.

Time passed, and after nine months the wife gave birth to a son, whom she named John. He grew up a happy boy, but at last the seven years were up, and the man said to his wife, "Now I must take John away, for it is him that I promised in exchange for the tablecloth."

At that his wife began to weep and rebuke him for being so foolish, but he said, "It cannot be helped. I must do it. I must go today."

There was nothing for it. The mother kissed her son good-bye, and the father led him though the wood and over the mountain to the little hut. There they found a table covered with a white tablecloth on which were set a bottle of wine and a loaf of bread; so they helped themselves.

The white-haired old man came in, and said, "You have come as you promised."

"Yes," said the man.

"That is good. If you had not come to me today, I should have gone to you tomorrow. And you have brought me your son. What is his name?"

"John."

"Has he had any education?"

"Only what I can give him myself."

"Well, do not worry. I shall give him a good education. I shall treat him as if he were my own son, and I shall make him a fortunate man."

The man had to be satisfied with that. He left John with the white-haired old man, and went back to offer his wife what words of comfort he could.

John grew into a strong handsome lad and stayed with the old man until he was quite grown up. Then the white-haired old man told him, "Today you and I are going to climb to the top of the mountain. Look above the door and you will find a horse's bridle. Bring it with you."

At the top of the mountain, the white-haired old man said, "John, shake the bridle at me, and I shall turn into a horse. Then you must leap on my back."

John did as he was told. He shook the bridle, and the white-haired old man turned into a fine horse with a white mane. John leaped on its back, and the horse set off at a terrific pace, never letting up whether the ground was hard or soft until they came to the sea cliff. There was a big cave there, and the horse said, "Get off my back, John, and go into that cave. You shall find three giants lying down in it, dying of hunger. If you look in my ear you shall find something to help them." John looked in the horse's ear and found a bottle of wine and three loaves of bread. "Give them a loaf each, and a swig of wine," said the horse. "And while they are eating and drinking, ask them to remember the help you have given them."

John did as he was told. When the giants were refreshed, they thanked him and he said, "I hope you will remember the help I have given you."

"Perhaps we will," said the chief giant.

Then John went back to the horse and rode down onto the beach, where the horse told him to get down. "On the beach you will find a great fish, dying for want of water. Help it back into the sea, and ask it to remember the help you gave it."

John did as he was told. When he asked the fish to remember him, it answered, "Perhaps I will."

Then John got back on the horse, and they rode on until they came to a great castle made of burnished bronze. The horse said, "Get off my back, John, and go into the brazen castle. You shall see rooms full of gold and rooms full of silver, but by all you hold dear do not touch any of it. Just look around and come back to me."

John did as he was told. He passed through rooms full of gold and rooms full of silver, but he did not touch any of it. However, when he was coming out of the castle he did see a large bundle of goose feathers, and he took one of those to make himself a pen.

When he got back to the horse, it asked him whether he had had a good look around.

"I did," said John.

"And you did not touch anything or take anything?"

"No," said John, for he did not count the goose feather.

"Leap on my back," said the horse.

They rode off again until they came to the castle of the king. "Get off my back, John," said the horse, "and go and ask if the king needs a clerk."

John did so, and found that the king did want a clerk to work for his head clerk. John went out and told the horse, who said, "Accept the job until you get a better. Should any trouble come upon you, think of me, and I will come to you."

So John took service with the king as a clerk. Everything was to his liking except the pens that they used. So remembering the goose feather he had taken from the brazen castle, he made a quill pen of it. When he wrote with that quill, his writing was so beautiful that everyone remarked on it, even the king.

They asked John where he had got the pen, and he told them that he had got it from the brazen castle.

"I thought that must be the case," said the king. "As you have dared to go once into the brazen castle, you must go twice. For I have decided to marry the lady of the brazen castle, and you must go and bring her to me."

"I cannot do that," said John.

"You must do it, or you shall be hanged," said the king.

John went to his room and began to weep. "If only the white-haired old man were here," he said to himself.

A moment later the white-haired old man came into John's room. "What is the matter?" he asked.

John told him what the king had said to him, and the white-haired old man said, "You must have touched something in that castle, although I told you not to."

"I didn't touch anything," said John. "Only a feather, which I made into a pen. Though indeed it is that pen that has brought this trouble on me."

"Touching a feather was as bad as touching the silver or gold," said the white-haired old man. "I told you not to touch anything. However, come with me and we will see what can be done."

The old man turned into a horse, and they went to the shore, from where they could see the brazen castle further along the coast. The white-haired old man gave John a rod and said, "Strike me with the rod, and I shall become a ship full of silk. Sail up to the brazen castle and anchor there, and then row over to the castle in the skiff and do exactly as I tell you, and all shall be well."

John turned the old man into a ship, and sailed up to the castle. Then he rowed up to the castle in the skiff, and just as the old man had predicted the lady of the castle leaned out of an upper window and asked, "Where have you come from?"

"From the Indies," said John.

"With what cargo?" asked the lady.

"A cargo of silk," said John.

"Please bring some ashore to show me," said the lady.

"There is too much, and I do not know what would please you," said John. "As it is a mild day, why don't you come out to the ship?"

So the lady came out of the castle and got into the skiff with John, and he rowed her out to the ship and showed her the bundles of silk that were below the deck.

They spent a long time looking at the silk, and when at last they came up on deck the ship was well out at sea.

"What have you done to me?" said the lady.

"Nothing for you to fear," said John.

"I see that I have lost my brazen castle," she said. She put her hand in her pocket and took out the keys of the castle. "Whatever happens to me, no one shall enter my home," she said; and she threw the keys into the sea.

John took the ship ashore at the point from which he had set out, and struck it with a rod, so that it turned into the white-haired old man, and then again, so that he turned into a horse. Then he set the lady on the horse and went up to the king's castle.

The next morning John went back to work as a clerk, while the king told the lady of the brazen castle that he wished her to marry him. "I shall never marry you until you bring the brazen castle here and add it on to the palace," she said.

"We must make John do it," said the king. He sent for John, and said to him, "You must fetch the brazen castle here and add it to the palace, or else you shall be hanged."

John went up to his room. "Only the white-haired old man can save me now," he told himself.

Then the old man came into his room. "What is the matter now?" he asked, and John told him. "I told you not to touch anything in that castle. This is all your own fault," said the old man. "However, come with me, and we shall see what we can do."

The old man turned back into a horse, and they rode to the cave of the giants. "Go in, and remind them of the day you gave them bread and wine," said the old man.

John went into the giants' cave. He said to the chief of the giants, "Do you remember the day when you were dying of hunger, and I came in and gave you bread and wine?"

"I think such a thing may have happened," said the giant.

"Well if you are ever going to remember it," said John, "I hope that you will remember it today."

"What do you want?" asked the giant.

"I want you to fetch the brazen castle and add it to the king's palace," said John.

"Perhaps I will," said the giant.

John went down to the white-haired old man and told him what the giant had said. "That is as good as a cast-iron promise," said the old man, and they went back to the king's palace.

Next morning when the king rose, he found the brazen castle added onto his palace. But the door was locked, and he could not get in. When he asked the lady of the castle to marry him, she said, "I shall never marry you until I get the bundle of keys that I threw into the sea."

The king said, "We will make John get them." And he told John that he must get the keys, or be hanged.

Once again John went to his room and called on the white-haired old man, and once again he came. "Now the king wants me to fetch the keys to the brazen castle from beneath the sea," said John.

"I told you not to touch anything in that castle," said the old man. "Still, come with me, and we shall see what we can do."

The old man turned into a horse, and they rode down to the beach. "Call on the king of the fish," said the old man, "and remind him of the day when he was stranded on the beach by the receding tide, and you helped him back into the water."

So John went to the water's edge and called to the king of the fish, and he came. John asked him, "Do you remember the day when you were stranded here by the tide, and I helped you?"

"I do," said the great fish. "What do you want?"

"I want you to fetch me the keys to the brazen castle from the bottom of the sea," said John.

The king of the fish went away and was gone for a long time. But when he came back, he had the keys. John thanked him and went back to the old man.

They returned to the king's palace, where John gave the keys to the king, and the king gave them to the lady.

"Now will you marry me?" said the king.

"I shall never marry until I get three bottles of water from the well of virtues," said the lady.

"I cannot get them for you," said the king. "We must make John get them."

So once again John went back to his room and called on the white-haired old man for help.

"I know I should never have touched anything in the brazen palace," he said, "but if you do not help me, I shall be hanged."

"Well," said the white-haired old man, "come with me, and we shall see what we can do."

The old man turned back into a horse, and they rode a long way from the castle. And then the horse said, "Get down from my back, John. Find a good lump of stone, and strike me at the root of my ear, and kill me. Five ravens will come to feast on my body. You must steal out your hand and catch two of them. The other three will beg you to release their brothers, and you must say, 'Not until you fetch me five bottles of water from the well of virtues.' The ravens will bring you water, but you must make sure that they do not trick you. Pour some of the water on my body. If it is the right water, I shall rise up alive and well. If it is not, I shall not stir."

Everything happened as the horse predicted. John killed him. the ravens came, and the three free ravens fetched five bottles of water. But when John poured the water on the horse's body, it did not stir. So he squeezed the two captured ravens even more tightly, saying, "I will throttle them to death if you do not bring me the right water."

Then the three free ravens set off again, and this time they were gone for a long while. When at last they reappeared with five more bottles, John poured some on the horse's body, and this time it rose up alive and well, so John let the ravens go free.

John leaped on to the horse, and they rode back to the castle. On the way, the horse said, "Give away three bottles of the water, John, but keep two; and if you need me, think of me."

John gave the three bottles of water from the well of virtues to the king, who gave them to the lady of the brazen castle. She poured the water into a cauldron and set it on a fire to boil. When the water was boiling, she leaped into the cauldron and washed herself from head to toe with the water from the well of virtues. She said, "I shall never marry any man who cannot stand in the boiling water as long as I can."

So the king jumped into the cauldron with her, and was scalded to death.

John thought of the white-haired old man, and he came. John told him what had happened.

"First take the water from the other two bottles and wash yourself from head to toe," said the old man. "Then you will be able to stand the boiling water in the cauldron. But do not get in before the lady has promised to marry you."

So John washed himself in the water from the well of virtues, and then he said to the lady, "If you will marry me, I will leap into the cauldron with you."

"I will marry you," she said, and he leaped into the cauldron, put his two arms around her, and began to kiss her.

"You are my man now," she said.

So John and the lady got out of the cauldron, and the white-haired old man married them there and then and made John king in place of the one who had died. Then the old man said, "Good-bye, John. I have done what I promised your father and made a fortunate man of you." And he went away and was never seen again.

But if John and the lady have not died since then, they are alive still.

THE LITTLE BIRD

MANY YEARS AGO in Ireland there was a very holy man, one of the monks in a monastery. One day when he was in the garden of the monastery he was so overcome with the beauty of this world that he fell down on his knees to thank God.

As he prayed, he heard the song of a little bird from one of the rose trees in the garden, and it was the most lovely song he had ever heard—as joyous as a sunbeam and as liquid as a stream. He rose from his knees to listen to the heavenly sound.

The bird flitted from tree to tree, and the holy man followed it. He felt he would never tire of listening to it.

The bird flew far, far from the monastery, and still the holy man followed it, enchanted by its sweet song.

At last the bird fell silent, and the holy man knew it was time to return.

As he walked back to the monastery, the sun set over the hills in a glory of red and gold. By the time he arrived, it was nightfall.

When he got home, the holy man found everything strange. The monks walking here and there were unknown to him; the buildings seemed altered; even the garden where he had knelt to pray was different.

He stopped a monk and asked him, "Brother, what is the meaning of all these changes that have taken place here since this morning?"

"What do you mean?" asked the monk. "Nothing has changed. And

who are you? You wear the habit of our order, but I do not know you."

The holy man told the monk his name, and how he had fallen to his knees to pray that morning and then wandered away from the garden following the heavenly song of the little bird.

And the monk said, "There is a tradition here that, two hundred years ago, a brother of your name disappeared from the garden and was never seen again."

The holy man replied, "Then I see that my hour is come. God has granted me a glimpse of heaven on earth, and now my soul must depart."

So the holy man made his confession to the monk and received absolution, and then he died.

For the little bird was an angel, sent by God to lead the holy man to heaven.

THE TAIL

A SHEPHERD ONCE went out to the hill to look after his sheep. It was misty and cold, and it was hard work finding them. At last he had them all but one. After much searching he found that one too, half drowned in a peat hag—a marshy hollow where he had cut peats from the moor to burn on his fire.

The shepherd took off his coat, bent down, took hold of the sheep's tail, and he pulled!

The sheep was heavy with water, and he could not lift her. So he took off his plaid, bent down, took hold of the sheep's tail, and he *pulled!*

But it was too much for him. So he spit on his hands, bent down, took hold of the sheep's tail, and he PULLED!

And the tail broke!

If the tail had been stronger, this tale would have been longer.